Leading Toward Efficacy

Leading Toward Efficacy

Why Cognitive Coaching Persists

By
Arthur L. Costa and Robert J. Garmston

BLOOMSBURY ACADEMIC
NEW YORK • LONDON • OXFORD • NEW DELHI • SYDNEY

BLOOMSBURY ACADEMIC

Bloomsbury Publishing Inc, 1359 Broadway, New York, NY 10018, USA
Bloomsbury Publishing Plc, 50 Bedford Square, London, WC1B 3DP, UK
Bloomsbury Publishing Ireland, 29 Earlsfort Terrace, Dublin 2, D02 AY28, Ireland

BLOOMSBURY, BLOOMSBURY ACADEMIC and the Diana logo are trademarks of
Bloomsbury Publishing Plc

First published in the United States of America 2025

Copyright © Bloomsbury Publishing, 2025

Cover design by Kathi Ha
Cover images © iStock.com/HRAUN

All rights reserved. No part of this publication may be: i) reproduced or transmitted in any form, electronic or mechanical, including photocopying, recording or by means of any information storage or retrieval system without prior permission in writing from the publishers; or ii) used or reproduced in any way for the training, development or operation of artificial intelligence (AI) technologies, including generative AI technologies. The rights holders expressly reserve this publication from the text and data mining exception as per Article 4(3) of the Digital Single Market Directive (EU) 2019/790.

Bloomsbury Publishing Inc does not have any control over, or responsibility for, any third-party websites referred to or in this book. All internet addresses given in this book were correct at the time of going to press. The author and publisher regret any inconvenience caused if addresses have changed or sites have ceased to exist, but can accept no responsibility for any such changes.

Library of Congress Cataloging-in-Publication Data is available

ISBN: HB: 978-1-5381-9822-3
PB: 978-1-5381-9823-0
ePDF: 979-8-7651-5460-1
eBook: 978-1-5381-9824-7

Typeset by Deanta Global Publishing Services, Chennai, India

For product safety related questions contact productsafety@bloomsbury.com.

To find out more about our authors and books visit www.bloomsbury.com and sign up for our newsletters.

Contents

Foreword *Diane Zimmerman* — vii
Acknowledgments — x
Introduction — xi
    Don't Get in Over Your Head: The Allure of Adaptive Leadership — xi
    Five Capacities of Efficacious Leadership — xviii

Section I Cognitive Coaching: Reflections

Introduction — 2

1. **Cognitive Coaching: Promising Results** *Jenny Edwards* — 3
   Part 1: Eleven Outcomes of Implementing Cognitive Coaching — 4
   Part 2: Nineteen Recommendations for Implementing Cognitive Coaching — 16
2. **Philogelos: Something We Left Out** — 29

Section II Relevance in an Emerging World

Introduction — 34

3. **Cognitive Reflection and Neurodiversity**
   Diana Rosberg and Bridget McNamer — 37
4. **Developing Leaders' Efficacy . . . Virtually**
   Kendall Zoller and Michael Tonkin — 45
5. **Diversity Matters: Creating and Sustaining Systems of Belonging** *Phil Echols, Stacie L. Stanley, and Delores B. Lindsey* — 53

6 **Leading with Prosocial and Emotional Intelligence** *Wendy Baron* — 61

Section III Applications of Cognitive Coaching's Principles and Values in Other Disciplines

Introduction — 70

7 **Enhancing Mind-Body Awareness** *EJ Zebro and Bena Kallick* — 71
8 **Cognitive Coaching in Spiritual Accompaniment** *Father Luis J. González* — 79
9 **Coaching in Health Care** *John Clarke* — 87
10 **Coaching and Teaching Vocal Music** *Sue Pressler* — 97
11 **Elevating Learning: Merging Education and Business Practices** *William Sommers* — 103

Section IV Enduring Values and Deepening Learning

Introduction — 114

12 **Cognitive Coaching in Retrospect: Why It Persists** — 115
13 **"Thinking Makes It So": Students as the Authors of Their Life Script** *Laura Lipton and Steve Jambor* — 129
14 **Humility and Humanity** — 141

Glossary — 149
Further Reading — 153
Index — 154
About the Contributors — 159

Foreword
Diane Zimmerman

When we come to understand our own personal operating principles, we have the power to change our world and influence others. It is through our personal efficacy that we impact entire communities and develop collective efficacy—a world-worthy focus for our future.

In the 1980s, Arthur Costa and Robert Garmston designed an educational coaching model that explored the power of metacognition. At that time, most administrators were anointed to supervise and evaluate teachers, yet few had been trained in "the how" of instructional supervision. In response, Art worked to perfect a course on instructional supervision and soon partnered with Robert Garmston who added his knowledge of psycho-communicative aspects of leadership.

Together they formed an alliance and invited me to join them as a practitioner to test their ideas in real school settings. Out of this partnership grew Cognitive Coaching. For school leaders looking for powerful ways to improve instruction, Cognitive Coaching offered key concepts that began to shape our practices of coaching and leading. In the 1980s and 1990s, Cognitive Coaching filled a leadership void in schools and the group of trainers expanded exponentially.

Those of us who committed to the practices of Cognitive Coaching applied many of the principles to aspects of our professional lives. We shared stories of how these newfound patterns of facilitation increased our positive agency—the ability to produce positive results for teachers and students. As coaches, we noticed how language patterns became internal thinking processes and built efficacy—the conviction of personal agency. We were discovering that the consistent use of language patterns supported others' metacognition. Over and over, coaches reported, "I am not fixing problems, I am using my words to invite others to solve their own problems."

In 1994, Art and Bob wrote a comprehensive summary of this work in their book, *Cognitive Coaching*. They continued to set their coaching model apart from others with their metacognitive rather than a behavioral approach to supervision. Instead of directing clients, the cognitive coach challenged the client to frame and analyze their own problems of practice. In response the coach applied a discrete set of language tools to facilitate the conversation. The focus was on thought processes specifically heightening consciousness, expanding options, fostering craftsmanship, seeking interdependence, and building efficacy. Out of this came a set of language patterns for coaches to use to enhance thinking about our thinking called "states of mind." These five states of mind framed specific language around efficacy, consciousness, flexibility, craftsmanship, and interdependence.

We were not an easy group and often challenged Art and Bob and each other to go deeper and really question our intentions. Collectively, we were wary of directive, top-down behaviorist approaches. We also cared about excellence and were committed to producing tangible results. As a result, we found the tenants of Cognitive Coaching transferable to many aspects in our professional lives. Bob Garmston and Bruce Wellman wrote about these extended understandings in their 1999 book *The Adaptive School*.

The first book documented the "what and why" of Cognitive Coaching and has stood the test of time. But, as so is often the case, our ideas are sometimes overshadowed by more scripted behavioral approaches to coaching. For those in a rush to solution, the idea of directing others seems more expedient. Unfortunately, these models often inhibit the honest reflection needed to produce deep understanding. While well intended, no degree of outside standard setting will ever quite establish excellence. That is because excellence comes from within, when we come to understand that how we operate in the world has the power to change our worlds—when we become both personally and collectively efficacious—we can articulate how we produce intended results.

Adding to this legacy, Art and Bob's protégés adopted this metacognitive approach to coaching and spent their lives adapting the tools to fit professional contexts. Now, thirty years after the publication of the first edition of the book, we want to reflect and project forward to ask ourselves, "What are the *enduring concepts* in our work, worthy of informing practices into the future?" In this book, we compile these enduring concepts and summarize a set of core principles about human metacognition as important today as they were over forty years ago.

We offer our wisdom gleaned over our careers, learning in collaborations that led us to understand universal truths about how we can work together in the name of compassion, compromise, and communication—all necessary goals for the future. Through understanding each other, we find enduring concepts and an ability to think and work through differences so that we can continue to grow and learn together. In the spirit of Cognitive Coaching, we offer no fixes. Instead, we focus on essential concepts and in the writing create "thought spaces" that are dynamic and fluid. We invite the reader to enter a dialogue with us about how to expand the human capacity to make helping relationships more robust and to develop a professional canon, not just about coaching but for other domains of human communication.

What is needed now, more than ever, is a set of enduring concepts from which our leaders can celebrate the wisdom gained from careers spent testing and adapting. Indeed, in this conflicted world, we think this metacognitive stance allows us to stand outside of ourselves and to look in at our own thoughts, to consider other's thoughts, and to find ways to explore common understandings. Our world today is more complex, more conflicted, and more distracted than the world in which these ideas were conceived. Yet, we believe we offer a language of practice that is attuned to meeting the psychological and metacognitive needs for this next generation.

–Diane Zimmerman, January 18, 2024

Acknowledgments

This book could not exist without the tireless and extraordinary work of Cat Costa-Jones. From the outset of this project, she has instructed and guided the authors and advised their efforts at understanding and working with advancements in today's advanced computer and communication technology. Her contributions made it even possible that these authors, both in their nineties, could even conceive of beginning this book.

Cat brings her exceptional skills as a journalist, operations manager, and knowledge of sensitive public relations to the sometimes-delicate job of guiding and encouraging chapter authors and others involved in creating this book. We are honored to dedicate this work to Cat and are immeasurably grateful for this opportunity to work with her.

Art and Bob
August 2025

Introduction

Don't Get in Over Your Head: The Allure of Adaptive Leadership

Adaptive leadership is a style of leadership introduced by Ronald Heifetz and Marty Linsky (Heifetz & Linsky, 2017) to address complex, long-term problems or challenges. It can also help organizations adapt to change. Leaders who govern collaboratively must be comfortable in causing discomfort for teachers, and perhaps their community while they simultaneously provide psychological safety and be open to questioning their own behavior and theories of teaching and leadership. These "holding environments" are sheltered states in which teachers are supported, while at the same time required to practice and develop the new skills a program requires.

This chapter will reveal distinctions between adaptive and technical change and describes processes necessary for the former. Because adaptive change may be enticing to consider but daunting in practice, leaders should be forewarned regarding some necessary challenges. Heifetz et al. (2009) captured an understanding of adaptive change thus: "Challenges requiring adaptive change are created by a gap between a desired state and a reality . . . that cannot be closed using existing approaches alone."

Traditional, hierarchical views of leadership are less and less useful given the complexities of our modern world. Leadership theory must transition to new perspectives that account for the complex adaptive needs of organizations. In this chapter, we propose that leadership (as opposed to leaders) can be seen as a complex dynamic process that emerges in the interactive "spaces between" people and ideas.

Complexity theory argues that certain interactions in a social network will have a nonlinear influence of future interactions. Eicholz believes that adaptive leadership requires first asking what the organization needs to change and, second, mobilizing people toward that change. Eicholz presumes most organizations are not capable of adaptive change. In the 1927 *Forbes* list of the largest companies, only nine remained in this list by 2014. One company, Kodak, whose story is familiar to many, was once the leading manufacturer and processor of photographic film. But during the onset of digital photography and cell-phone cameras, it was unable to evolve with the changing technology. This cautionary tale feels eerily familiar in 2025 as many teachers are wondering how to adapt to new technology like AI. What, we ask, will be involved in turning AI into a useful instructional tool?

The essential question for each school is, "What is our adaptive challenge?" That is, what is it we must begin doing and end doing? What skills and competencies do we need to develop in order to achieve adaptive change (Garmston & Wellman, 2005)?

> The world is moving at such a rapid pace that control has become a limitation. It slows you down. You've got to balance freedom with some control, but you have to have more freedom than you've ever dreamed of. (Jack Welch, CEO of General Electric)

Adaptive change requires learning and developing new ways of thinking and behaving over time. Command and control systems of management are well suited for technical work, like revising a district's routing of its buses, but fails with adaptive work.

The speed of introduction of new technologies, introductions of new curriculums, and pressures from parents and community require a constant need for change. But that change requires equilibrium that must be reached through a process that sustains tensions while requiring tension to change. Readers might recall an example from their own experience.

If leadership is not "in" a leader or "done by" a leader, however, how are we to insightfully conceive exactly what constitutes leadership and from where it originates? A novel approach for answering these questions is grounded in complexity science, namely the notion that *leadership is an emergent event*, an *outcome of* relational interactions among agents. In this view, leadership is more than a skill, an exchange, or a symbol—leadership *emerges through* dynamic interactions (Bradbury & Lichtenstein, 2000). "Complexity leadership theory" investigates the role of leadership in expediting those processes in organizations through which interdependent actions among many individuals combine into a collective venture" (Drath, 2001; Meyer et al., 2005).

> The complexity leadership orientation redirects emphasis away from an individual as leader. It does not ignore the importance of leadership as an organizational phenomenon; "rather, it recognizes that leadership transcends the individual by being fundamentally a system phenomenon (Marion & Uhl-Bien, 2001; Hazy, 2006).
>
> Inferred by complexity science, complexity leadership theory offers a new perspective for leadership research. This theory considers leadership within the framework of the idea of a complex adaptive system (CAS).

Wellman and Garmston characterize these systems as ones in which tiny events produce major outcomes. Everything affects everything else, and you don't have to touch everyone to make a difference. In this case, relationships are not primarily defined hierarchically, but rather by *interactions* among heterogeneous agents and across agent networks.

Leaders considering adaptive change address these questions:

1. What must be done to enable the conditions within which the interactive processes necessary for adaptive change occur? Or, how much adaptive capacity does my organization have and how might its capacity be increased?
2. What tools exist supporting collaborative ownership of challenges and resolution development?[1]

Murray Gell-Mann (1997) offers this perspective:

> As one century transits to another, the network of relationships linking the human race to itself and to the rest of the biosphere is so complex that all aspects affect all others to an extraordinary degree. Someone should be studying the whole system, however crudely that has to be done, because no gluing together of partial studies of a complex nonlinear system can give a good idea of the behavior of the whole.

Gell-Mann's observation characterizes adaptive change as a process of making small, incremental adjustments to address complex challenges that are difficult to identify and may not have an obvious solution. It's a process that involves new learning, experimenting with new approaches, and a cultural shift in values and beliefs.

When members try, without success, to adopt new procedures in adaptive efforts, the leader's role is to support persons attempting the new patterns with encouragement while simultaneously making it clear that persons must continue to learn and try until they succeed at the new processes. This is not negotiable. Eichholz calls this a "holding environment" (2016).

What's Involved in a Change of This Magnitude?

Achieving potential long-term solutions can involve experimenting with new approaches and practices. Adaptive changes typically require a collective effort and a cultural shift in values, beliefs, attitudes, and approaches. Adaptive change can take some time to fully implement and requires an ongoing process of thoughtful strategy, ongoing learning, and collective support. The only way to test a proposed approach is to use it and evaluate results. One of the authors of this book once initiated some collaborative approaches. Developmental changes occurred over a four-year period. From an accepted reading program for fourth to sixth grade students, teachers managed three reading groups per period to a program of fifty-minute teacher-led instruction for a single group, resulting in reduced teacher stress and improved student-reading gains.

The principal and key teachers overcame resistance from faculty, the assistant superintendent of instruction, the school board, and the teacher union's decision-making members. Unknowingly this venture was influenced by lady luck, organizational change literature of the time, and passionate engagement of principal, teachers, and key parents. However, knowing what we now know, neither author would approach this without considerable thoughtfulness, research, and trepidation.

The Adaptive School by Garmston and Wellman (1999) describes essential skills that we now understand as prerequisites to adaptive attainment. Leaders are encouraged to ask if their operation holds enough of these. Reflecting on the reading program transformation above, many of the following skills and concepts were developed and reinforced throughout the project to provide chances for adaptive change to occur. Central to these are distinguishing dialogue from discussion, interpersonal communication skills, effective meeting management, and with the necessary skills, seeing conflict as opportunity rather than something to be ignored.

Contrasting Technical with Adaptive Change

Technical changes are made in response to clearly defined issues or challenges. These solutions are relatively straightforward, and the leaders or experts within an organization can usually address them without consulting the rest of the company. For example, if the internet goes out in a school, this is a straightforward problem with a straightforward solution. To address this, the principal and maintenance workers follow practiced procedures. Leaders make technical changes in a short time frame, and people are usually receptive to the change or solution.

Illustrating Technical and Adaptive Change

Metaphorically, one can, with difficulty yet with reasonably possible effort, locate the beginning and ending of each strand on a ball of rubber band. On the globe representing the world, and adaptive change, strands are entangled, pulling one, affecting others, and neither the beginning of the strands can be located nor their endings. In these dynamic systems, everything affects everything else (Garmston & Wellman, 2005).

1. More data does not lead to better solutions.
2. Tiny events create major disturbances. Remember the kid that was absent last week?
3. You don't have to touch everyone to make a difference.
4. Both things and energy matter.

All above, below, and upon us are dynamic systems placing a wisp of cloud there, sunlight there, or winds you need to cover from. So, too, is your school subject to these forces. Tread carefully.

Humans live, of course, within dynamic systems. What's the weather like where you are today? Do you have clouds, clear skies, rain, hail, snow, or hurricane force winds? Is this the umpteenth day you've had temperatures over 100 degrees Fahrenheit? Some communities are experiencing water shortages. What is a shortage you remember, if any?

Tension Drives Programs

Tension is a driver of adaptive leadership. A second driver of innovation in adaptive leadership events occurs when the interactions between agents spark tensions that lead to adaptive change. When agents interact, they may experience tension in the form of pressure on and challenges to their personal knowledge base. Often that leads to adaptive change.

Heifetz observes that progress for adaptive change requires more than the application of current expertise, authoritative decision-making, and standard operating procedures. He points to several special characteristics:

- distinguishing between what is precious and essential, and what is expendable
- accepting that adaptive work demands experimentation
- accepting that adaptive work requires running multiple experiments and learning fast to see "which horses to ride into the future"
- remembering that in adaptive change, small events make major disturbances, and everything affects everything else.

Heifetz observes that people resist loss, not change. Going through adaptive change requires many losses. A process of grieving occurs. The mandate for a leader who is leading a community through adaptive change, then, is to hang in there with them while they work their way through adaptive change. Leaders must construct a holding environment (Eichholz, 2016).

Figure I.1 Technical change (left, rubber bands); adaptive change (right, globe).

Holding Environments

A holding environment is a psychological space that is both safe and uncomfortable. For example, when we certify trainers in Cognitive Coaching, Adaptive Schools, or Habits of Mind, we create a holding environment in which team teaching initially occurs. Pairing a novice with a veteran trainer, coplanning, coteaching, and coreflection happen. In this space, the novice can test new ways of being with the support and guidance of an experienced trainer, and we have witnessed tears and insights in these collaborations as former mindsets are set aside (Garmston, 2018, pp. 129–137).

Eicholtz (2016) offers this example: A father or mother helping a kid learn to ride a bike requires a holding environment. The helpful dad or mom runs alongside a kid learning to ride a bike. The kid is safe in that the parent is there to catch her if failure occurs. But the kid is uncomfortable, Eicholtz observes, because she is the one doing the work—the balancing, the pedaling, and the steering. She is the one learning the new behavior. If the parent is holding onto the bike, the parent is doing the work. But if the parent is only there with outstretched arms not quite touching the kid or the bike, then it's a holding environment.

Avoiding Adaptive Work

Heifetz talks about two ways that people avoid doing adaptive work. They don't do adaptive work when they don't feel the problem strongly enough. And they don't do adaptive work when they feel the problem too strongly—that is, when they feel crushed by the weight of the problem. We once worked with a veteran fourth-grade teacher would have seen him as bright with no commitment. We coplanned, cotaught, and coassessed, and started the cycle again with coplanning. He tended to perform well when we were with him. When we removed the holding environment, however, his support fell as did his performance.

Leaders must develop ways to adjust the environment. turning up the heat so that it becomes more uncomfortable and turning down the heat so that it feels safer. Shielding teachers from unreasonable central office demands is one example. (One of the authors was once told to develop a bicycle safety program for his school. What was he to do? Conduct fewer classroom visits to make time for this project? Or turn the project over to parents? He chose to do the latter, and they did an excellent job.)

Make people feel "the pinch of reality" says Eicholtz. Reality is painful because each person really does need to change. The pinch of reality refers to the negative consequences that come from not changing. We turn up the heat, he says, by helping people feel the pinch of reality so that they can discover the problem for themselves. What might we do to turn down the heat? Heifetz points out that one way to make people safer is to focus for a brief time on technical problems. So, for example, the parent could spend time focusing the kid on how to pedal, all the while holding on to the bike. Then, the child builds back the confidence to keep pedaling.

Relating this concept closer to home, many have parents reaching an advanced age. Mom and dad lose their younger vigor and may lose familiar activities like hiking or golfing. At some point, they must endure the loss of driving. Perhaps there is loss of hearing or seeing capacity declines. Grief is a natural response to the loss of their autonomy or physical abilities. People don't resist change—*they resist loss*.

Keagan and Leahy (2009) observe that when we experience the world as too complex, we are not just experiencing the complexity of the world—we are experiencing a mismatch between the world's complexity and our own at this moment. There are only two logical ways to mend this "mismatch": reduce the world's complexity or increase our own.

In this book, we asked practitioners from other disciplines how Cognitive Coaching principles and skills might appear in their own work. You will find examples of their responses in Sections II–IV.

In Conclusion . . .

"Getting old ain't for sissies," our grandparents said. Adaptive change, too, is equally demanding and disorienting and must be developed with foresight, patience, and planning.

Five Capacities of Efficacious Leadership

Efficacious leading is essential for organizations to achieve their goals and to fulfill their mission. Leaders contribute to a positive and supportive culture where others are inspiring and empowering groups and individuals to achieve success and make a lasting impact on the lives of students and the communities they serve.

Leadership has long been confused with the notion of hierarchical positions, authority, power, and influence. While efficacious leadership may be associated with the level of confidence in the knowledge, skills, and abilities associated with leading others, what if we assumed that leadership is not a position (e.g., principal, captain, king, superintendent, chief, boss, director, CEO), but rather that leadership is a set of behaviors or interactions that all members of an organization could perform? Instead, leadership might be seen as a complex dynamic process that emerges in the interactive "spaces between" people and ideas. That is, leadership is a dynamic that transcends the capabilities of individuals alone; it is the product of interaction, tension, and exchange rules governing changes in perceptions and understanding (Lichtenstein et al., 2006).

Leadership invested in a single person, of course, continues in some organizations, perhaps most often in the corporate world. *The Harvard Business Review* remains a useful learning resource for solo leaders wishing to increase their efficacy. In a 2023 article titled "The Anxious Micromanager," neuropsychologist Julia DiGangi explored different management styles and the effect they have on the mental health of the workplace. One of the managers she spoke to pointed out, "Honestly, one of the most transformative things I've learned about leadership is the less I worry about controlling others, the more interested they are in following me." She observed that "realizing his command-and-control leadership style was not scalable to the smart dynamic organizations he wanted to lead."

Many corporate and educational institutions alike are reaching similar conclusions realizing that attributes of efficacious leadership are not role-bound, rather they often are functions of skillful teams. Each function listed below is an example of the five orientations, or macro-skills, of efficacious leaders. These five are capacities that all members of an organization are capable of learning and performing:

1. self-managing
2. self-monitoring

3. self-modifying
4. promoting self-efficacy in others
5. growing collective efficacy in teams

Self-Managing

> There's no leadership without self-leadership. To lead others, you must lead yourself... What is self-leadership? Some say there are three components: self-awareness of personal values, self-awareness of intentions and behavior, and self-awareness of your perspective. Self-leadership, at its core, is self-awareness.
>
> —Laurie Ruettimann

Self-managing refers to an efficacious leader's belief in their ability to regulate and control their own actions, words, emotions, and thoughts. It involves having intentionality—setting goals, making decisions, and taking responsibility for conduct. It means choosing to act and make proactive commitments, to taking action to change one's life and environment. It is defined as knowing the significance of and being inclined to approach tasks with clarity of outcomes, a strategic plan, and necessary data. It involves drawing from past experiences, anticipating success indicators, and creating alternatives for accomplishment.

Efficacious leaders have a sense of deliberativeness: They think before they act and regulate and control their own behavior, emotions, and thoughts. They intentionally form a vision of a product, plan of action, goal, or a destination before they begin. They strive to clarify and understand directions, develop a strategy for approaching a problem, and withhold immediate judgments before fully understanding an idea. As reflective individuals, they consider alternatives and consequences of several possible directions prior to taking action. They consider implications for themselves and the effects of their actions on themselves and on others. They decrease their need for trial and error by gathering information, taking time to reflect on an answer before giving it, making sure they understand directions, and listening to alternative points of view.

Self-Monitoring

> Your brain shall be your servant instead of your master. You will rule it, instead of allowing it to rule you.
>
> —Charles E. Popplestone

Mindful of *The Little Engine That Could* (Piper, 1930), efficacious leaders believe in their ability to plan and work toward completing a task and to achieve their goals. *"I think I can, I think I can, I know I can!"* They have confidence in themselves to control their behavior and remain motivated to achieve desired outcomes and to persevere even when faced with obstacles. They have the ability to act on their plans, to monitor their progress, and to make course corrections if they stray from their plan.

Self-monitoring requires awareness of their own thoughts, emotions, and behaviors, and evaluating them against personal values, goals, and standards. It means employing strategies and dispositions and searching for their effects on others and on the environment. It involves having sufficient self-knowledge about what works, establishing conscious metacognitive strategies to alert the perceptions for in-the-moment indicators of whether the strategic plan is working or not, and assisting in the decision-making processes of altering the plan and choosing the right actions and strategies.

Self-monitoring is the control and management of all cognitive resources also known as executive functioning. A simple example of this might be drawn from a reading task. It is a common experience while reading a passage to have our minds wander from the pages. We "see" the words, but no meaning is being produced. Suddenly we realize that we are not concentrating and that we've lost contact with the meaning of the text. We recover by returning to the passage to find our place, matching it with the last thought we can remember, and, once having found it, read on with connectedness. This inner awareness and the strategy of recovery are components of metacognition, or self-monitoring.

Having an internal dialogue (or self-talk) includes mental rehearsal, self-coaching, and listening to our "inner voice." This is what efficacious leaders use to reflect on what they do; how and why they do as they do; how they critique themselves; and how they connect the knowledge and ideas within their conceptual frameworks. It is the voice that challenges them to strive further and the voice that condemns their foolishness (Treadwell, 2014).

Self-Modifying

> A goal of education, therefore, is to assist growth toward greater complexity and integration and to assist in the process of self-organization—to modify an individual's capacity to modify themselves.
>
> —Reuven Feuerstein

For leaders, self-efficacy determines not only what goals are pursued and how those goals are accomplished but also how they reflect upon their own performance. Self-modification refers to the process of deliberately changing behaviors, thoughts, or feelings in order to improve themselves or their quality of life. It involves actively taking steps to create positive change and growth. As continuous learners, efficacious leaders draw upon past experiences and learn from their successes and failures.

Self-modifying means taking time to reflect on, meditate, evaluate, and give serious thought to their own behaviors, motivations, and desires in order to grow and improve. Meaning is made by analyzing feelings as well as data, comparing results with expectations, finding causal factors, and projecting ahead to how these insights may apply to future situations. Self-modifying implies making a commitment to learn from and to employ those insights and meanings autonomously in future events and situations.

Promoting Self-Efficacy in Others

> Leadership is about making others better as a result of your presence.
> —Sheryl Sandberg

Promoting self-efficacy in others means creating conditions which motivate and empower others to develop their full potential, to self-direct, and to fulfill the organization's mission. They encourage colleagues to set and achieve goals, and they lead by example by sharing their own goals. This modeling includes risk-taking and considering failures and successes as opportunities to learn. To build others' self-efficacy requires leaders to provide opportunities for others to take leadership and to live efficacy as an organizational value.

Growing Collective Efficacy in Teams

> My approach is to be in tune with the people with whom I'm working. I can see in the musicians' bodies and faces how they're feeling that day, and it becomes very clear who may need encouragement and who may need cautioning. The objectivity and perspective I have, as the only person who is just listening, is a powerful thing. I try to use this perspective to help the ensemble reach its goals.
> —Michael Tilson Thomas, music director, San Francisco Symphony

To grow collective efficacy, leaders recognize and acknowledge the impact of the work environment on the status and actions of others. In 1993, Bandura noted that collective efficacy is a social resource that does not get depleted by its use; it gets renewed. He referred to this as "reciprocal causality."

Collective teacher efficacy is a teacher team's shared belief that by working together, they foster high student achievement across a school in ways that individuals cannot. It's been well documented that teams with a high sense of collective teacher efficacy have a strong likelihood of positively impacting student learning. In a 2011 meta-analysis of studies, Rachel Eells illustrated that the beliefs teachers hold about a school's environment, attitudes, and abilities are "strongly and positively associated with student achievement across subject areas and in multiple locations" (p. 110). Confirming the findings in Eells's research, John Hattie listed collective efficacy as the number one factor that influences student achievement. Fascinatingly, he concluded that collective efficacy was more powerful and predictive of student achievement than socioeconomic status, prior achievement, home environment, parental involvement, student motivation and concentration, persistence, and engagement (2016).

Collective teacher efficacy doesn't just happen. Rather, it occurs when encouraging teams of educators to set, collaborate toward, and attain shared goals related to teaching and learning. During this process, the team's sense of empowerment increases, and stronger social cohesion between team members elicits a sense of collective teacher efficacy.

Much like a music director, efficacious leaders gather data by observing others' voice, tone, body language, facial expressions, interactions, mindsets, and reactions to both positive and adverse situations. This level of attention requires the efficacious leader's ability to be present and empathetic toward others, actively listening and responding to their needs and emotions. In well-functioning organizations, empathy is a two-way street. A leader's vulnerability makes clear their role as a peer, not a boss. Teaching teachers these same skills can dramatically accelerate the capacity of groups.

A striking example is the elite pilots of the US Navy Blue Angels Flight Demonstration Squadron, probably the most efficacious of teams. These heroes create a culture of gratitude by expressing appreciation for each other's contributions. They have built a culture that leaders can emulate, valuing trust, continuous learning, attention to detail, humility, and gratitude, which each pilot expresses by saying, "Glad to be here," It reminds each and every team member that what got them there was earned, not given to them and that keeping their spot should never be taken for granted. This motto serves as a daily reminder of their privilege to be part of the organization and can help push them to believe in themselves and their teammates (Yaeger, 2024).

In Conclusion

Efficacious leadership is a journey, not a destination. It's about constantly learning and growing and adapting. These principles offer a powerful model—not mandate—for leaders who want to make a significant impact.

> In the last analysis, what we are communicates far more eloquently than anything we say or do.
>
> —Stephen Covey

Note

1 See *The Adaptive School: A Sourcebook for Developing Collaborative Groups*, Chapter 3: Developing Collaborative Norms, Chapter 4: Two Ways of Talking, Chapter 5: Conducting Successful Meetings, Chapter 6: Designing Time Efficient and Effective Meetings, and Chapter 8: Using Conflict as a Resource.

References

Bandura, A. (1993). Perceived self-efficacy in cognitive development and functioning. *Educational Psychologist, 28*(2), 117–148.

Bradbury, & Lichtenstein. (2000). *Complexity leadership theory*. Charlotte, NC: Information Age Publishing.

DiGangi, J. (2023, August 22). The anxious micromanager. *Harvard Business Review*. https://hbr.org/2023/09/the-anxious-micromanager

Drath, W. (2001). *The deep blue sea: Rethinking the source of leadership* JOSSEY-BASS.

Eells, R. J. (2011). *Meta-analysis of the relationship between collective teacher efficacy and student achievement* (Doctoral dissertation). Loyola University Chicago. https://ecommons.luc.edu/luc_diss/133

Eichholz, K. F. (2016, December 11). *Adaptive capacity: How organizations can thrive in a changing world.* Lid Pub Inc.

Garmston, R. (2018). *The art of professional learning* (pp. 129–137).

Garmston, R. J., & Wellman, B. M. (1999). *The Adaptive School*. Norwood, MA: Christopher-Gordon.

Garmston, R. J., & Wellman, B. M. (2005). *The adaptive school: A sourcebook for developing collaborative groups* (2nd ed.). Lanham, MD: Rowman & Littlefield Publishers.

Garmston, R. J., & Wellman, B. M. (2016). *The adaptive school: A sourcebook for developing collaborative groups* (3rd ed.). Lanham, MD: Rowman & Littlefield Publishers.

Gell-Mann, M. (1997, October 12–November 10). The simple and the complex. International Society for the Systems Sciences, The Primer Project. http://www.isss.org/primer/gellman.htm

Hazy, J. K. (2006). Measuring leadership effectiveness in complex socio-technical systems. *Emergence: Complexity & Organization, 8*(3), 58–77.

Heifetz, R. A., Grashow, A., & Linsky, M. (2009). *The practice of adaptive leadership: Tools and tactics for changing your organization and the world.* Harvard business press.

Heifetz, R., & Linsky, M. (2017). *Leadership on the line, with a new preface: Staying alive through the dangers of change.* Harvard Business Press.

Hattie, J. (2016, July). *Mindframes and maximizers.* 3rd Annual Visible Learning Conference held in Washington, DC.

Kegan, R., & Lahey, L. (2009). *Immunity to change: How to overcome it and unlock the potential in yourself and your organization.* Harvard Business Press.

Lichtenstein, B. B., Uhl-Bien, M., Marion, R., Seers, A., Orton, J. D., & Schreiber, C. (2006, November 1). Complexity leadership theory: An interactive perspective on leading in complex adaptive systems. *Digital Commons at University of Nebraska Lincoln, Management Department Faculty Publications.* https://digitalcommons.unl.edu/managementfacpub/8/

Marion, R., & Uhl-Bien, M. (2001). Leadership in complex organizations. *The Leadership Quarterly, 12*(4), 389.

Meyer, A., Gaba, V., & Colwell, K. (2005). Organizing far from equilibrium: Nonlinear change in organizational fields. Organization Science, 16: 456–73.

Piper, W. (1930). *The little engine that could.* Platt & Munk.

Treadwell, M. (2014). *Learning: How the brain learns.* Auckland, N.Z. www.MarkTreadwell.com/products

Yaeger, D. (2024, August 1). Leadership lessons from the Blue Angels. *Chief Executive.* https://chiefexecutive.net/leadership-lessons-from-the-blue-angels/

Section I

Cognitive Coaching: Reflections

Introduction

In 2003, we wrote an article entitled "Cognitive Coaching in Retrospect: Why It Persists." Eighteen years after its inception, Cognitive Caching was still growing. It was being used in international schools, its concepts and skills were being applied in other support functions like consulting and facilitation, educators were requesting to be trained as Cognitive Coaches because of supportive nature of the work which honored independence and self-directed learning.

Cognitive Coaching first saw light in the February 1985 issue of *Educational Leadership*. We expressed our earliest thoughts about cognition, teaching, and supervision. We described the "invisible" cognitive processes of instruction—what happens inside a teacher's head prior to, during, and after teaching. We suggested that changing perceptions and cognition were prerequisite to enhancing instructional behaviors and we suggested coaching interventions intended to engage and transform teacher's thinking.

Eighteen *more* years of work on Cognitive Coaching have occurred since that first article, and now—nearly *forty years* into this journey—development has continued, and applications are emerging and growing in leadership, mentoring, and peer coaching.

But why, at year eighteen, was the program so strong, growing stronger, and sought by more educators? At that time, we reasoned that the following factors were responsible: detailed knowledge in the disciplines of cognition, teaching, and human relations, researched results, and clarity regarding the metacognitive skills of coaching. When we reported this to associates, they indicated that we were partially right but had missed the most consequential reason of all:

"Heart," they said.

People are drawn to Cognitive Coaching because, at essence, it is a restorative practice, offering support without judgment, encouragement for self-directed learning, relationship on equal levels and practical and observable results. The coach is as much a beneficiary as the person being coached.

In this section, we introduce a fresh perspective on the importance and role of efficacy and its relationships to the states of mind consciousness, flexibility, craftsmanship, and interdependence. Dr. Jenny Edwards also brings us a comprehensive look at current research findings, relating Cognitive Coaching to fields beyond education, efficacy, and worker collaboration.

Cognitive Coaching
Promising Results

Jenny Edwards

Part 1: Eleven Outcomes of Implementing Cognitive Coaching (p. 4)

Summary (p. 15)

Part 2: Nineteen Recommendations for Implementing Cognitive Coaching (p. 16)

Summary (p. 22)

Editor's Note: Dr. Jenny Edwards, in many ways a Cognitive Coaching (CC) conscience for the forty years since its conception, has served the invaluable role of observing, checking, and keeping a continuous record of the growing body of evidence of CC's applications and results. She published the nineteenth report regarding CC's results and promises in 2025. In this case, she begins by offering readers an examination of the promising results of implementing CC. This is followed by a series of recommendations, followed by a summary of references. In addition to providing regular reviews of CC studies, she has worked closely with Luis J. González (see his chapter "Cognitive Coaching in Spiritual Accompaniment" in Section

II of this book), the Catholic priest who advanced this work in parts of the church. She and Father Luis introduced CC in Italy, Spain, the Philippines, and Latin America. The CC community, practitioners, and trainers are forever in her debt.

–Robert J. Garmston

Part 1: Eleven Outcomes of Implementing Cognitive Coaching

What are some of the reasons to implement Cognitive Coaching? What are some of the benefits it will bring to my organization? How will coaching help my employees improve their practice? What are some of the ways that those in the system will benefit?

These are all important questions, the answers to which are revealed in research. Researchers have found the following in the field of education:

1. Successful induction into the field through Cognitive Coaching
2. Higher levels of implementation of innovations as a result of professionals receiving Cognitive Coaching, which resulted in gains for students
3. Increased efficacy in professionals
4. Increased ability to reflect and think in complex ways
5. Increased satisfaction with position and choice of profession
6. More professional cultures
7. Increased collaboration
8. Growth as professionals
9. Personal benefits
10. Benefits for administrators
11. Benefits for professionals outside of education
12. Eleven outcomes of implementing Cognitive Coaching

Over the years, researchers have conducted over 115 studies on Cognitive Coaching. Garmston and Hyerle (1988) and Donnelly (1988) did the first studies. Garmston and Hyerle studied a peer coaching program in which professors learned to use Cognitive Coaching, and Donnelly examined the processes administrators used as they were implementing Cognitive Coaching. In 1989, Foster found that teachers thought they grew cognitively as a result of using Cognitive Coaching. In 1993, Edwards built on her study. Even though teachers thought they grew cognitively, did they actually grow?

She found that they did. In addition, she found that they grew in their ability to reflect.

Since then, researchers have investigated the results of using Cognitive Coaching to help teachers in training and to help teachers implement innovations. They have studied its effect on teacher and administrator efficacy, as well as on teacher and administrator reflective thinking. In addition, they have explored teacher satisfaction with their position and with their choice of teaching as a profession, the professionalism of school cultures, and teacher collaboration. Researchers also found that Cognitive Coaching benefited teachers both professionally and personally, and that it benefited administrators and people in fields other than education.

This chapter includes information about some of the studies with implications for other professions. For synopses of all of the studies on Cognitive Coaching, please go to www.thinkingcollaborative.com and click on About Us . . . Research. Then, scroll down to *Cognitive Coaching: A Synthesis of the Research* and click on Read More. The pdf file of the book will download.

Outcome #1: Successful induction into the field through Cognitive Coaching

While many studies on Cognitive Coaching have been done with students and teachers, the outcomes have implications for a broader population. Some of the studies were focused on providing Cognitive Coaching to people who were new to the profession of teaching (Göker, 2020; González Del Castillo, 2015; Wilcoxen et al., 2020) or new to being an administrator (Rogers et al., 2016). In these studies, Cognitive Coaching was helpful. Four of the studies appear below.

In a ten-week study, Göker (2020) compared thirteen student-teachers who received Cognitive Coaching with thirteen student-teachers who did not receive Cognitive Coaching. Those who received Cognitive Coaching were more student focused and had higher expectations of them. They also increased in their awareness of the importance of analyzing what their students needed.

González Del Castillo (2015) provided Cognitive Coaching to three teachers who were new to the profession. The teachers then used Cognitive Coaching skills with their students, who increased in their ability to think deeply. In addition, the teachers became more responsible to students and increased in confidence. They believed their coaches were focused on meeting their needs, and they developed feelings of increasing ownership of what they were doing. They felt active rather than passive because they were participating in coaching conversations rather than attending seminars.

Wilcoxen et al. (2020) analyzed the qualitative responses of 438 teachers, 341 of whom were new teachers, who had participated in the Career Advancement and Development of Recruits and Experienced (CADRE) Teachers Project to learn about how the project had impacted them. The project included Cognitive Coaching. The teachers reported that they had felt empowered with an increased sense of well-being. When they were feeling overwhelmed and trying to survive, the fact that Cognitive Coaching was nonjudgmental enabled them to develop trust and reflect on how they were thinking. They reported that the program had supported their self-directedness, resiliency, and capacity to reflect on their practice.

Rogers et al. (2016) created the Leader2Leader (L2) Leadership Pilot Program in Alberta, Canada, to help new principals. Fifteen experienced principals who had been trained in Cognitive Coaching provided coaching to twenty-three incoming principals for sixteen months. As a result, student test scores increased in ten schools and remained the same in eight of the schools. These studies might suggest that Cognitive Coaching can support professionals who are coming into a field.

Outcome #2: Higher levels of implementation of innovations as a result of professionals receiving Cognitive Coaching, which resulted in gains for students

Studies have also shown that when professionals receive Cognitive Coaching to assist them in implementing innovations, they will implement them at higher levels. This will result in gains for those they serve. In a key study, Joyce and Showers (2002) found that when teachers studied theory and watched demonstrations, they did not implement what they learned. When they practiced what they had learned, they implemented 5 percent; however, when they received peer coaching, they implemented 95 percent of what they had learned. The following researchers, among others, have found that when people received Cognitive Coaching after attending seminars, they implemented it at a higher level: Akyildiz and Semerci, (2016), Alicea (2014), Batt (2010), Diaz (2013), Irons (2014), and Rennick (2002).

Akyildiz and Semerci (2016) used reflective teaching along with Cognitive Coaching for seven weeks with thirty students at the university level who were learning to speak English. They compared their findings with students who had learned English through lectures. They discovered that the students who had received Cognitive Coaching to help them learn English grew significantly more than the comparison group, and they retained what they had learned three weeks later at a significantly higher level.

Alicea (2014) studied nine teachers and forty-four paraprofessionals who were learning to use a protocol with their students (Sheltered Instruction

Observation Protocol (SIOP)). They attended twelve seminars over a period of two years. Alicea "found that post-implementation as a measure of cognitive coaching was a statistically significant predictor of the ESL [English as a Second Language] teachers' and ESL paraprofessionals' knowledge of SIOP" (p. 97). In addition, "as ESL teachers' and ESL paraprofessionals' knowledge of SIOP increased, their use of SIOP in their classrooms also increased" (pp. 97–98).

In a study by Batt (2010), fifteen teachers who had received instruction in the SIOP were provided with Cognitive Coaching sessions to assist them in implementing it. Prior to receiving coaching, 53 percent of the teachers had implemented the model "to a great extent," while after coaching, all of them had implemented it "to a great extent" (p. 1003). After receiving coaching, the teachers indicated that they noticed positive effects on what students were learning. Batt concluded "that coaching has a direct and significant effect on teachers' instruction. The cognitive coaching phase heightened implementation substantially, even after teachers had already had an extended period of long-term ongoing training and peer collaboration in each school" (p. 1004). In addition, the teachers found that student achievement improved "as a result of heightened SIOP implementation following the coaching phrase, which both rewarded teachers for employing the framework and further motivated them" (p. 1005).

Diaz (2013) also found that Cognitive Coaching helped teachers implement what they learned at higher levels. She taught teachers of grades 2 through 5 elements of the National Board Certification in Group One and Group Two, while Group Three did not receive any intervention. Group One received 8–10 Cognitive Coaching sessions in four months in addition to what they learned about the National Board Certification, while Group Two only learned about National Board Certification and did not receive Cognitive Coaching. The students of teachers in Group One increased in their achievement scores more than the students in the other two groups. In addition, Grochocki (2018) found that "self-efficacy is directly affected by cognitive coaching processes and bears a strong relationship to passing the National Board Certification" (p. 83).

Irons (2014) investigated the outcomes when teachers attended a seminar on asking mediative questions and then received coaching for ten weeks as they expanded their use of questioning in the classroom. She found that the participants placed value on the coaching they received. They also went from asking closed-ended questions to asking open-ended questions. They believed they had learned from the seminar and the coaching. They had taught the new skills to their students, and they had implemented what they learned into their practice.

In a similar study, Rennick (2002) compared test scores of students of kindergarten teachers who had attended a two-week lecture course on providing a balanced literacy program for their students. One group received Cognitive Coaching to assist them in implementing what they had learned, the second group did not receive Cognitive Coaching, and the third group neither received the training nor the coaching. Students of teachers in the Cognitive Coaching group had significantly higher test scores on the Gates-MacGinitie Reading Test, Level BR (Beginning Reading) (MacGinitie et al., 2000). These findings might suggest that after professionals have taken seminars on innovations they will need to implement, Cognitive Coaching could help them to deepen their knowledge and implement the innovations at higher levels, resulting in benefits for those they serve.

Outcome #3: Increased efficacy in professionals
Many researchers have studied the impact of Cognitive Coaching on the development of efficacy in educational professionals. The sample below includes studies on teacher efficacy (Göker & Göker, 2021; Sándigo, 2017; Wooten-Burnett, 2014) and administrator efficacy (Cox, 2021; Skytt et al., 2014).

Göker and Göker (2021) studied six teacher candidates for fourteen weeks when they were learning to teach English as a Foreign Language (EFL) in Turkey. They found significant growth from pretest to posttest on the Teachers' Sense of Efficacy Scale (TSES) (long form) (Tschannen-Moran & Hoy, 2001). Qualitative data from discussions and participant journals confirmed the test scores.

Sándigo (2017) studied four college-level tutors who used Cognitive Coaching to coach ten Hispanic tutees for twenty-one weeks to increase their levels of academic English (AE). As a result, the tutors increased in self-efficacy, and those whom they tutored increased in "confidence to succeed academically" (p. iii).

Wooten-Burnett (2014) explored the development of the efficacy of seven teacher candidates in a master's program in physical education. They received three cycles of Cognitive Coaching, including three Planning Conversations and three Reflecting Conversations, for six weeks. She compared them with seven teachers in a control group. She found that "Cognitive Coaching had a statistically significant impact on physical education teacher candidates' teacher efficacy measured by the PETES (Physical Education Teaching Efficacy Scale, Humphreys et al., 2012) and OSTES (Ohio State Teacher Efficacy Scale, Tschannen-Moran & Hoy, 2001)" (p. 121). The teachers reported that the Planning Conversation enabled them to "become more aware of student needs" (p. 96). It also helped them to develop their ability to think critically, set expectations that were realistic, and increase in their flexibility. In addition, they learned to reflect on their lessons. They grew both personally and professionally, focused more on their lessons, and improved in their ability to plan lessons.

Cox (2021) conducted a study in which five principals received Cognitive Coaching for six weeks. "The school leaders... described feeling clearer, more confident, and better prepared for next steps after having Cognitive Coaching conversations with instructional coaches" (pp. 144–145). In conclusion, Cox reflected, "It cannot be said that the principals in this study have higher self-efficacy in general after having engaged in Cognitive Coaching, but each principal did raise their self-efficacy for the particular situation they chose to discuss with the coaches" (p. 133).

In a study by Skytt et al. (2014), fifteen experienced principals provided coaching for twenty-three new principals. While the experienced principals had significantly higher levels of efficacy on two of the subscales of the Principal Sense of Efficacy Scale (Tschannen-Moran & Gareis, 2004) at the beginning of the study, no differences existed between the efficacy of the coaches and those whom they coached after two years of coaching. These findings suggest that when professionals receive Cognitive Coaching, they tend to increase in efficacy.

Outcome #4: Increased ability to reflect and think in complex ways
Cognitive Coaching also has helped people to think at deeper levels about what they are doing. In fact, more researchers have discovered increased levels of reflection as a result of Cognitive Coaching than any other area of investigation. Between 1988 (Garmston & Hyerle, 1988) and 2023 (Hunter, 2023), forty-four researchers found that the participants in their studies increased in their abilities to reflect on their practice. Some researchers used instruments to measure increased ability to reflect, others shared their observations about the participants, while still others indicated that the participants reported having increased abilities to reflect.

Instruments measuring reflection on which participants who had received Cognitive Coaching grew significantly included the Metacognitive Awareness Inventory (MAI) by Schraw and Dennison (1994) (Hughes & Partida, 2020), the Reflective Attitude Survey by Young (1989) (Gomez, 2005), the Reflective Pedagogical Thinking Instrument (RPT) by Sparks-Langer et al. (1990) (Edwards, 1993; Moche, 1999, 2000), and the Teacher Thought Processes Questionnaire by Foster (Foster, 1989; Uzat, 1999). Other researchers used qualitative methods such as journals, interviews, focus groups, and self-designed surveys to assess participant reflection. Information about ten of the studies appears below.

In a study by Jaede et al. (2014) with twenty-eight middle school and high school mentor-teachers in urban schools who received Cognitive Coaching, the teachers moved from asking "How do students learn?" to asking more refined questions such as, "How will I ensure these students, in this classroom, in this school, in this community learn?" and "How does who I am in the context of my classroom impact learning?" (p. 27)

In Hunter's (2023) study, the increased reflection of the teachers in her study resulted in changes in the way they taught. When Walczak (2022) used the Cognitive Coaching model, the teacher in the study reflected and made modifications in instruction. Cox (2021) analyzed coaching conversations of principals and reported,

> All leaders spoke of stress and fatigue at some point, then after coaching, reached a place where they reported specific steps for problem solving, clear goals, empathy, and a feeling of relief and renewed confidence about the topics of their Cognitive Coaching conversations. (p. 135)

Cox concluded, "Cognitive Coaching afforded principals the space and time to observe, reflect, and align actions to beliefs" (p. 146).

Thirteen primary-level student teachers who received Cognitive Coaching for ten weeks shared that they had become more reflective as a result of receiving coaching (Göker, 2020). Grochocki (2018) coached teachers who were preparing for National Board Certification. Qualitative data showed that the teachers were able to meet the expectations of the National Board. In addition, "those who receive cognitive coaching are more likely to demonstrate the reflective thinking skills necessary to be successful in completing the National Board Certification process than those who are not offered cognitive coaching support" (Grochocki, 2018, p. 83). In another study in which the researcher used Cognitive Coaching and communities of practice to support teachers who were going to take National Board Certification, the teachers "became more self-reflective in their teaching practice throughout the semester of study" (Robinson, 2011, p. 34).

González Del Castillo (2015) used classroom observations and semistructured interviews to assess the outcomes of Cognitive Coaching. "Participants . . . pointed out the increase in their use of reflective practice" (p. 114). Participants also felt "empowered to use skills and practices they were familiar with, analyze them, modify them, and apply them in a new way as a result of their participation in the cognitive coaching cycles" (p. 115). In a study of 117 teachers at the elementary and secondary level who received training in Cognitive Coaching compared with 117 teachers in a comparison group who had not received the training, teachers in the treatment group grew significantly more than those in the comparison group in reflecting (Chang et al., 2014).

Bjerken (2013) conducted a study with elementary, middle school, and high school teachers in a school district to discover the impact of four years of Cognitive Coaching on their teaching. He based the findings on surveys and focus groups. Teachers reported that their ability to reflect had improved, and they felt less isolated. In addition, they were able to think in more detail about the lessons they taught. These findings suggest that when people engage in Cognitive Coaching, they can increase in their ability to reflect on deeper levels.

Outcome #5: Increased satisfaction with position and choice of profession
An early area of investigation focused on teacher satisfaction with their position and with their choice of teaching as a profession. Edwards et al. (1998) and Edwards and Newton (1994a, 1994b, 1995) learned that teachers who had taken training in Cognitive Coaching were significantly more satisfied with teaching as a profession than those in the comparison group. Teachers who had not been trained in Cognitive Coaching listed fifty-seven areas with which they felt dissatisfied as teachers, while those who had received Cognitive Coaching training only listed sixteen areas (Edwards & Newton, 1994a). Those trained in Cognitive Coaching mentioned the following sources of satisfaction more often than those not trained: the ability to learn and grow, changes in the profession, a chance to impact the lives of students, the opportunity to use their creative skills, and other staff members (Edwards & Newton, 1994a).

In a study by Clinard et al. (1995), teachers who worked with student-teachers using Cognitive Coaching indicated they had "renewed enjoyment and enthusiasm about teaching in the classroom" (p. 21). They also had more motivation to stay in education. Edwards and Newton (1994a) reported that teachers listed autonomy, flexibility, and the chance to make positive impacts on students' lives as sources of satisfaction. Teachers indicated they liked the fact that they could use the Cognitive Coaching skills in a variety of contexts, the process was nonjudgmental, coaching positively impacted school culture, they enjoyed coaching with their colleagues, it made sense to them, they had grown professionally, and they were able to reflect on their practice. In other studies, researchers found that teachers grew significantly in satisfaction with their positions from pretest to posttest as a result of participating in Cognitive Coaching (Awakuni, 1995; Edwards et al., 1998).

As a result of these findings, Edwards (2004) conducted a grounded theory study to discover the reasons Cognitive Coaching resulted in teachers having increased satisfaction with teaching as a profession and with their position. She had observed that more experienced teachers in the three-year million-dollar grant she had conducted on Cognitive Coaching went from reporting they were burned out from teaching and wanted to retire to saying they planned to stay in the profession for many years because of their renewed excitement for teaching. She found that teachers who reported enthusiasm for Cognitive Coaching were interested in "Becoming." The interviewees identified five steps in the process: "Beginning the Journey, Learning for Becoming, Gathering Colleagues on the Path, Re-Identifying, and Continuing the Journey" (p. 71). First, they began to learn about Cognitive Coaching because they were interested in growing and gaining skills to support others. In addition, Cognitive Coaching was aligned with their beliefs and values. Then, they sought out more opportunities to learn in order to benefit themselves and others. It was so enjoyable that they wanted others to experience what they had experienced, so they invited others to join them on the path. As a result, they took on new identities consistent with their new passion for teaching. Finally, they continued learning on the journey. These findings suggest that Cognitive Coaching can create renewal as well as increased energy, enjoyment, and satisfaction in professionals.

Outcome #6: More professional cultures
Teachers and principals felt more professional as a result of coaching or being coached as shown in the following studies (Awakuni, 1995; Clinard et al., 1997; Edwards et al., 1998; Reed, 2007; Skytt et al., 2014), as well as others. Awakuni (1995) noted that teachers who used Cognitive Coaching for a year gave more presentations, became more involved in state activities, and volunteered for leadership positions in the school. In a study by Clinard et al. (1997), supervising teachers reported they grew in their professionalism by using Cognitive Coaching with their student teachers.

Teachers who were trained in Cognitive Coaching increased significantly on the Teacher Professionalism and Goal-Setting subscale as well as the Administrator Professional Treatment of Teachers subscale of the School Culture Survey (Saphier, 1989) over a comparison group in a study by Edwards et al. (1998). Did the teachers who had received training in Cognitive Coaching believe their administrators treated them more professionally as a result of their feeling more professional, or did their administrators treat them more professionally because they were acting in a more professional manner?

Teachers in a study by Reed (2007) who received Cognitive Coaching had "a renewed sense of professionalism" (p. 231). This created "a more professional attitude," as well as "teachers' willingness to change their educational practice" (p. 231). When fifteen experienced principals coached twenty-three principals who were beginning their career for two years, school climate increased in the participants' schools (Skytt et al., 2014). Based on these studies, Cognitive Coaching may be one way to create more professional cultures in organizations.

Outcome #7: Increased collaboration
In addition to fostering increased professionalism, Cognitive Coaching training resulted in teachers collaborating more, as shown in studies by Dougherty (2000), Edwards et al. (1998), Edwards and Green (1997), Edwards and Newton (1994b), and Eger (2006), among others. Teachers trained in Cognitive Coaching felt less isolated, had a greater sense of trust, and felt more collegial in a study by Dougherty (2000). In three other studies, teachers also reported increased collaboration (Edwards et al., 1998; Edwards & Green, 1997; Edwards & Newton, 1994b). In another study, "there was a strong conviction that cognitive coaching was responsible for developing deeper and stronger relationships with [teachers] peers, as well as with their students" (Eger, 2006, p. 57). The teachers reported that they collaborated more, listened on deeper levels, were more patient with other teachers as well as with their students, and appreciated other teachers more. Cognitive Coaching may provide a way to increase collaboration among professionals.

Outcome #8: Growth as professionals
Cognitive Coaching also helped teachers to grow professionally. Grochocki (2018) reported that "that cognitive coaching builds and strengthens the ability of [National Board Certification] candidates no matter where they are in the process of certification" (p. 83). In a study of eighty-one teachers and eleven administrators in which the principals used Cognitive Coaching, slightly more than half shared that they thought the coaching conversations assisted the teachers in growing (Peery, 2022). In another study, teachers who received coaching felt affirmed in their abilities as teachers (Bowen, 2021). Freeman-Mack (2020) learned that twelve of the sixteen teachers in her study "felt the coaching meetings positively influenced their teaching ability and they were motivated to try something new in their instruction" (p. 92).

Göker (2020) compared thirteen primary student-teachers who received Cognitive Coaching for ten weeks with thirteen student-teachers who did not receive Cognitive Coaching. The teachers who received Cognitive Coaching indicated they grew in their identity as teachers, and they gained increased skills in writing lesson plans. In the study by Jaede et al. (2014) of twenty-eight middle and high school mentor-teachers who taught in an urban area, the teachers gained the identity of "teacher educators, mediators of intern learning" (p. 23). They also developed the identity of teacher leaders who collaborated with their colleagues as well as with parents and students.

Reed (2007) found that teachers who received Cognitive Coaching tried new teaching methods. In addition, they indicated their instruction had changed as a result of the coaching they received. Coy (2004) studied a program lasting a year in which mentors coached protégés. The protégés became more self-directed, and they moved from just making it through the day to focusing on helping their students succeed. In another study, first-grade teachers indicated they became more focused in their teaching, planned in a more thoughtful manner, became more craftsman-like, and questioned the way things had always been done (Slinger, 2004). Based on these findings, Cognitive Coaching appears to help people to grow professionally.

Outcome #9: Personal benefits
While personal growth was not initially a stated goal of Cognitive Coaching, some of the studies in which participants have mentioned it appear below. Professionals shared they had grown personally as a result of taking the eight-day training in Cognitive Coaching in studies by Beltman (2009) and Rogers et al. (2016). In Göker's (2020) study, participants who received three coaching cycles indicated "they became more aware of their self-development" (p. 574). They grew more flexible, became more aware of the need to set goals and use their critical thinking skills, and improved in confidence. In addition, teachers who were involved in Cognitive Coaching for a year indicated they had more self-confidence and more of a sense of self (Awakuni, 1995). Clinard et al. (1995) found that teachers felt more positively about themselves, and they changed their attitudes toward people in their families. Teachers who had received training in Cognitive Coaching and used it listed their top source of satisfaction as their ability to use the skills in a variety of areas of their lives, and they mentioned the #2 source of satisfaction as their ability to grow personally (Edwards & Newton, 1994a). In a study by Wooten-Burnett (2014), participants who received Cognitive Coaching reported the coaching "helped them become more aware of their self-development" (p. 97). It also assisted them in growing personally. Thus, Cognitive Coaching appears to benefit participants personally as well as professionally.

Outcome #10: Benefits for administrators
Cognitive Coaching provided benefits for administrators by helping them grow in their roles. Pavlock (2023) found that five K-12 educational leaders moved from giving information to being mediators of thinking as a result of taking training in Cognitive Coaching and using it for a year. In addition, the leaders became more vulnerable, more authentic, and more service-oriented.

They were more aware of themselves, had more humility, and were more intentional in their work and their interactions with others.

In studies by Lim (2016) and Lindle (2016), leaders supported others by asking more open-ended questions as a result of being trained in Cognitive Coaching. Rogers et al. (2016) used Cognitive Coaching with 23 new principals for 16 months. They felt "better prepared and more confident" to do their work, and they reflected more and were able to think "in more complex ways" (p. 22). They also felt "more satisfied at choosing to become a principal" (p. 22). In addition, the participants reported benefits for students, parents, and teachers in their schools. They explained that their school climates had become more positive, and teachers in their schools collaborated more. In a study by Ellison (2003) in which twelve principals and four assistant principals received coaching, participants reported "that this was one of the most valuable professional development experiences in which they had ever engaged" (p. 23). In addition to the many benefits provided by Cognitive Coaching, it can provide benefits for leaders.

Outcome #11: Benefits for professionals outside of education
Two researchers have studied Cognitive Coaching in fields other than education. Cognitive Coaching provided benefits for priests, nuns, and lay people in a program based on Cognitive Coaching in Rome, Italy, in a study by González (2009). He examined the Five States of Mind in relation to the spiritual life using a survey adapted from the Five States of Mind Scale for Cognitive Coaching (Ushijima, 1996). The group that participated in eight days of Cognitive Coaching training and received coaching two times a month for eight months showed the most growth in the Five States of Mind. Participants who had not taken the training and were coached two times each month grew the next most, and those who only participated in the eight-day training and did not receive coaching grew the next most. Participants who did not receive any of the interventions either stayed the same or regressed in the Five States of Mind.

Liebmann (1993) studied human resource developers who worked for service and product organizations. Participants indicated that the States of Mind of Consciousness and Interdependence, and then Flexibility, were important for everyone in the organization to have. These studies suggest that people outside of the field of education can receive benefits from Cognitive Coaching.

Summary

Numerous researchers have studied Cognitive Coaching since Garmston and Hyerle (1988) and Donnelly (1988) conducted the first studies, and each researcher has built on the work of those who came before. In the years since its inception, Cognitive Coaching has transformed the lives of administrators and teachers around the world by making them more efficacious, more collaborative, more professional, and more successful in educating students. The findings in the field of education have implications for other fields. If Cognitive Coaching can assist educators in making these changes, what might it be able to do for organizations outside of education?

Part 2: Nineteen Recommendations for Implementing Cognitive Coaching

What are some of the factors that leaders in an organization should consider as they are implementing Cognitive Coaching? How can leaders ensure maximum return on their investment? What conditions need to be present in a system in order to maximize the impact of Cognitive Coaching? Who should be trained, and what kinds of support might people in the organization need during the implementation process?

These questions are important for leaders to consider as they are designing a plan for bringing Cognitive Coaching into the culture of an organization. Researchers have identified the following nineteen recommendations as being critical for implementing Cognitive Coaching in a system.

1. Establish long-term system-wide support to provide training and support employees as they are implementing Cognitive Coaching
2. Enlist managers in supporting and modeling Cognitive Coaching
3. Be aware of implementation concerns and use tools such as the Concerns-Based Adoption Model (CBAM) Stages of Concern and Levels of Use when implementing Cognitive Coaching
4. Recognize that all employees can benefit from being involved in Cognitive Coaching
5. Create norms of collaboration
6. Develop a climate of self-directedness
7. Invite voluntary participation
8. Establish a trusting environment
9. Emphasize the importance of reflection
10. Create a climate of learning in the organization
11. Emphasize the importance of developing the identity of a mediator of thinking
12. Involve employees right away in using their coaching skills

13. Structure time for Cognitive Coaching
14. Recognize that employees tend to use Cognitive Coaching skills on an informal basis more frequently than the formal Planning Conversation, Observation, and Reflecting Conversation
15. Invite employees to use their coaching skills in many contexts
16. Distinguish between coaching and evaluating
17. Realize that policies in the larger environment can influence employees' adoption of the identity of a mediator of thinking (i.e., a Cognitive Coach)
18. Realize that other initiatives can help to develop the Five States of Mind in employees
19. Assign Cognitive Coaches with expertise in a particular area to others with expertise in those areas

Recommendation #1: Establish long-term system-wide support to provide training and support employees as they are implementing Cognitive Coaching

In order to implement Cognitive Coaching successfully, administrators need to support the initiative by providing funding, training, and other materials (Bair, 2017). Leaders will benefit by putting their goals in writing so that employees will know what is expected of them (Freeman-Mack, 2020). According to Reed (2007), three to five years are necessary for Cognitive Coaching to become part of the culture. In addition, if a union is present, leaders must involve them early in the process. Johnson (1997) found that administrators must commit to implementing Cognitive Coaching over a period of time for it to be successful, and they need to take a systemic focus. When administrators use Cognitive Coaching in meetings, people in the organization will be able to see its value and know the leaders view it as a priority.

Recommendation #2: Enlist managers in supporting and modeling Cognitive Coaching

When managers support Cognitive Coaching and use it in meetings, those in organizations will be able to observe their commitment (Freeman-Mack, 2020). Participants in a study by Tennison (2015) mentioned the importance of managers supporting Cognitive Coaching and using coaching with those in the organization. In a study by Edwards and Green (1999b), when teachers had the support and modeling of their principal, they persisted in a three-year project longer than teachers in schools in which the principals did not take the training. McLymont (2000) and McLymont and da Costa (1998) also found the importance of principal support in the success of the implementation of Cognitive Coaching.

Recommendation #3: Be aware of implementation concerns and use tools such as the Concerns-Based Adoption Model (CBAM) Stages of Concern and Levels of Use when implementing Cognitive Coaching

Reed (2007) found that when people adopted Cognitive Coaching, they went through the Stages of Concern and Levels of Use of the Concerns-Based Adoption model (Hall & Hord, 2001). This model was developed to examine how educators were implementing innovations. In the Stages of Concern model, people are first unconcerned about a new model. Then, they want to gain information about it. After that, they have personal concerns and wonder how it will impact them. Then, they want to find out how they can manage the model. Subsequently, they are concerned with the consequences of adopting the model. After that, they are interested in collaborating with others. Finally, they adapt it to meet their needs.

In the Levels of Use model, people go from not using an innovation to wanting to be oriented to it. Next, they prepare to implement it. On the next level, they use it in a mechanical manner. Then, they use it routinely. After that, they refine what they are doing. Then, they integrate the new model into what they were already doing. According to Reed, coaches need to explain the process of Cognitive Coaching and the types of conversations they will be having so that people being coached will understand the process.

Recommendation #4: Recognize that all employees can benefit from being involved in Cognitive Coaching

All employees can benefit from experiencing coaching. Researchers found that all teachers could benefit from Cognitive Coaching, whether male or female (Alseike, 1997) or the number of years they had taught (Alseike, 1997; Eger, 2006; Foster, 1989). In the study by Eger, no differences existed between teachers with regard to the grades they taught, how long they had been in the school district, and how long they had used Cognitive Coaching. Foster found no differences between teachers who taught at the elementary or secondary level.

Recommendation #5: Create norms of collaboration

Leaders can encourage people to use Cognitive Coaching by creating norms of collaboration among employees (Tennison, 2015). "Deeply embedded Cognitive Coaching environments work to build team mentality skills. Team mentality skills . . . include the critical tools of paraphrasing, pausing, and probing questions" (p. 92). Johnson (1997) observed that school buildings and school cultures tend to isolate teachers in their classrooms. Thus, leaders need to be aware of the physical setup of the building(s) in which employees work and create conditions in which people can collaborate.

Recommendation #6: Develop a climate of self-directedness
"The mission of Cognitive Coaching is to produce self-directed persons with the cognitive capacity for excellence both independently and as members of a community" (Thinking Collaborative, 2022, p. 16). Tennison (2015) found that "self-direction emerged as the second most important component in implementing a deeply embedded Cognitive Coaching environment, just after the component of establishing a collaborative culture" (p. 103). She also found that when leaders focused on building the "internal resourcefulness" of employees, they encouraged people to be self-directed (p. 105). If the mission of Cognitive Coaching is to encourage people to work in a self-directed manner, it can be helpful for leaders to foster self-directedness in a variety of ways.

Recommendation #7: Invite voluntary participation
As with any initiative, employees need to be able to choose whether they will become involved or not (Krpan, 1997; Smith, 1997; Weatherford & Weatherford, 1991). People tend to resist adopting initiatives when they do not perceive they have choice.

Recommendation #8: Establish a trusting environment
Coaches need to establish trusting relationships with people whom they are coaching (Freeman-Mack, 2020; Lindle, 2016; Netolicky, 2016a, 2016b; Reed, 2007; Tennison, 2015; Weatherford & Weatherford, 1991). In Tennison's study, participants mentioned the importance of trust eighty-five times. The nonjudgmental behaviors used in Cognitive Coaching contribute to the development of trust (McLymont, 2000; McLymont & da Costa, 1998; Netolicky, 2016a, 2016b; Reed, 2007). Mackenzie (2017) found that coaches need to hold what their coachees say in confidence in order to maintain trust. Coaches also need to establish trusting relationships in the larger organization (Johnson, 1997).

Recommendation #9: Emphasize the importance of reflection
In order to successfully implement Cognitive Coaching, leaders will benefit from emphasizing the importance of reflection (Tennison, 2015). When leaders talk about reflection, model it, and provide employees with opportunities to reflect, employees will develop a culture in which they reflect on what they are doing. Lane (2016) studied principals who coached 51 first-year or second-year principals. She found that when the coaches engaged in deep reflection, they were able to facilitate deep reflection in the people they were coaching.

Recommendation #10: Create a climate of learning in the organization

In addition, leaders can create a climate of learning in the organization. Tennison (2015) found that "deeply embedded Cognitive Coaching environments understand that organizational learning is the catalyst that moves an entire organization forward" (p. 107).

Recommendation #11: Emphasize the importance of developing the identity of a mediator of thinking

While many trainings provide skills for people to use, the goal of Cognitive Coaching is "to develop one's identity and capacity as a mediator of thinking" (Thinking Collaborative, 2022, p. 29). The development of a person's identity differs from just developing skills. Tennison (2015) found that people implementing Cognitive Coaching need to have the identity of a mediator of thinking. She shared that "all humans have their own journey in developing an identity as a Cognitive Coach" (p. 128). When people have the identity of a mediator of thinking, they will be more likely to use Cognitive Coaching than if they did not have that identity.

Recommendation #12: Involve employees right away in using their coaching skills

As with any new skill, employees will benefit from using their Cognitive Coaching skills right away (Edwards & Green, 1999b). In another study by Edwards and Green (1999a), those who used their skills immediately persisted longer in a three-year project. The more they practiced, the more skillful they became.

Recommendation #13: Structure time for Cognitive Coaching

If leaders want their employees to use Cognitive Coaching, they must provide time for them to engage in coaching conversations (Coy, 2004; Freeman-Mack, 2020; Reed, 2007). Lack of time to coach tends to be a barrier to coaching (Aldrich, 2005; Beltman, 2009; Edwards & Newton, 1994a; Lindle, 2016; Peery, 2022; Schlosser, 1998). When employees have designated time to engage in coaching conversations, they will use their skills more.

Recommendation #14: Recognize that employees tend to use Cognitive Coaching skills on an informal basis more frequently than the formal Planning Conversation, Observation, and Reflecting Conversation

While Cognitive Coaching consists of the Planning Conversation, Reflecting Conversation, and Problem Resolving Conversation, employees will use their coaching skills on an informal basis more often than they use the formal conversations (Awakuni, 1995). In a three-year project in which Cognitive Coaching was used to help teachers implement an innovation in a school district, a participant reported that she transformed her relationship with her daughter who was in high school by coaching her rather than telling her what to do (S. Rogers, personal communication, March 16, 1996). She also used Cognitive Coaching with other family members. Many others who have completed training in Cognitive Coaching have shared similar stories.

Recommendation #15: Invite employees to use their coaching skills in many contexts
Leaders can also invite and encourage employees to use their coaching skills in a variety of contexts because the more they practice, the better they become (Aldrich, 2005). Aldrich studied participants who engaged in coaching on the internet and found they greatly enjoyed it.

Recommendation #16: Distinguish between coaching and evaluating
Sometimes the same person can be called on to both coach and evaluate employees. J. Ellison (personal communication, January 28, 1995) shared that, as a principal, she physically wore one hat when she was coaching teachers and another hat when she was evaluating them. She added that by coaching teachers throughout the year, they received higher evaluations than if she had not coached them.

Weatherford and Weatherford (1991) found that leaders can coach and evaluate employees only as long as employees know when they are being coached and when they are being evaluated. The behaviors must be distinct. In a study by Freeman-Mack (2020), people being coached had more trust in the coach when they knew the coach wanted to assist them rather than evaluate them. She suggested developing a booklet to explain what people can expect from a coach.

Recommendation #17: Realize that policies in the larger environment can influence employees' adoption of the identity of a mediator of thinking (i.e., a Cognitive Coach)
Leaders who wish to implement Cognitive Coaching in their organization should be mindful of the immediate environment as well as the larger environment (Mackenzie, 2017). What values do leaders communicate in those environments? Do those values support the adoption of Cognitive Coaching, or do they mitigate against it?

Recommendation #18: Realize that other initiatives can help to develop the Five States of Mind in employees
Leaders can be mindful of ways in addition to Cognitive Coaching to develop the Five States of Mind of efficacy, flexibility, interdependence,

consciousness, and craftsmanship in their employees. Kilver (2017) found that teacher preparation courses could assist teachers in this area. What other initiatives might help employees to develop the Five States of Mind and work in conjunction with Cognitive Coaching?

Recommendation #19: Assign Cognitive Coaches with expertise in a particular area to others with expertise in those areas
When coaches have expertise in the areas of the people whom they are coaching, the people being coached will tend to have more respect for them and view them more positively than if the coaches did not have similar areas of expertise (Freeman-Mack, 2020). Thus, it would be important for leaders to assign coaches to people who have similar areas of responsibility and backgrounds.

Summary

Numerous researchers have discovered conditions that enable leaders to implement Cognitive Coaching. First, leaders need to commit to implementing Cognitive Coaching in the organization and engage everyone in supporting it. They need to create norms of collaboration and self-directedness, and they need to establish a trusting environment. When employees have time to use Cognitive Coaching and are encouraged to use their developing skills right away, they will implement it more quickly. It would also be important for leaders to examine the entire environment to ensure that it supports Cognitive Coaching.

References

Akyildiz, S. T., & Semerci, Ç. (2016, October). The Cognitive Coaching-supported reflective teaching approach in English language teaching: Academic and permanence success. *Academic Journals: Education Research and Reviews, 11*(2), 1956–1963.

Aldrich, R. S. (2005). *Cognitive Coaching^{SM} practice in online environments* (Publication No. 3197394) [Doctoral dissertation, Pepperdine University]. ProQuest Dissertations and Theses Global.

Alicea, R. (2014). *Influence of SIOP Cognitive Coaching workshops on teaching practices of ESL teachers and ESL paraprofessionals* (Publication No. 3646942) [Doctoral dissertation, Wayne State University]. ProQuest Dissertations and Theses Global.

Alseike, B. U. (1997). *Cognitive Coaching: Its influences on teachers* (Publication No. 9804083) [Doctoral dissertation, University of Denver]. ProQuest Dissertations and Theses Global.

Awakuni, G. H. (1995). *The impact of Cognitive Coaching as perceived by the Kalani High School core team* (Publication No. 9613169) [Doctoral dissertation, The Union Institute]. ProQuest Dissertations and Theses Global.

Bair, M. A. (2017, September). Faculty development through Cognitive Coaching. *New Forums Press, 31*(3), 79–85.

Batt, E. G. (2010). Cognitive Coaching: A critical phase in professional development to implement sheltered instruction. *Teaching and Teacher Education, 26*, 997–1005. doi.org/10.1016/j.tate.2009.10.042

Beltman, S. (2009). Educators' motivation for continuing professional learning. *Issues in Educational Research, 19*(3), 193–211.

Bjerken, K. S. (2013). *Building self-directed teachers: A case study of teachers' perspectives of the effects of Cognitive Coaching on professional practices* (Publication No. 3564120) [Doctoral dissertation, Minnesota State University, Mankato]. ProQuest Dissertations and Theses Global.

Bowen, L. R. (2021). *Growing culture and capacity through dialogic practice: Lesson study in a distributed learning environment* (Publication No. 28645535) [Doctoral dissertation, Concordia University—Chicago]. ProQuest Dissertations and Theses Global.

Chang, D., Lee, C.-D., & Wang, S.-C. (2014). The influence of Cognitive Coaching on teaching reflection and teaching effectiveness: Taking teachers participating in formative teacher evaluation in elementary and secondary schools as examples. *Journal of University of Taipei, 45*(1), 61–80. https://doi.org/10.6336/JUT.4501.004

Clinard, L. M., Ariav, T., Beeson, R., Minor, L., & Dwyer, M. (1995, April). *Cooperating teachers reflect upon the impact of coaching on their own teaching and professional life* [Paper presentation]. American Educational Research Association, San Francisco, CA, United States.

Clinard, L. M, Mirón, L., Ariav, T., Botzer, I., Conroy, J., Laycock, K., & Yule, K. (1997, March). *A cross-cultural perspective of teachers' perceptions: What contributions are exchanged between cooperating teachers and student teachers?* [Paper presentation]. American Educational Research Association, Chicago, IL, United States.

Cox, J. H. (2021). *Space to lead: Cognitive Coaching as mindful school leader practice.* [Doctoral dissertation, University of Louisville]. Think IR: The University of Louisville's Institutional Repository. https://ir.library.louisville.edu/etd/3660/

Coy, L. J. (2004). *A case study of a professional development initiative focused on novice teacher mentoring* (Publication No. 3155974) [Doctoral dissertation, New Mexico State University]. ProQuest Dissertations and Theses Global.

Diaz, K. A. (2013). *Employing National Board Certification practices with all teachers: The potential of Cognitive Coaching and mentoring* (Publication No. 3557981) [Doctoral dissertation, Arizona State University]. ProQuest Dissertations and Theses Global.

Dougherty, P. A. (2000). *The effects of Cognitive Coaching training as it pertains to: Trust building and the development of a learning community for veteran teachers in a rural elementary school* (Publication No. 3054864) [Doctoral dissertation, University of Southern California]. ProQuest Dissertations and Theses Global.

Edwards, J. L. (1993). *The effect of Cognitive Coaching on the conceptual development and reflective thinking of first year teachers* (Publication No. 9320751) [Doctoral dissertation, The Fielding Institute]. ProQuest Dissertations and Theses Global.

Edwards, J. L. (2004). The process of becoming and helping others to become: A grounded theory study. In I. F. Stein, F. Campone, & L. J. Page (Eds.), *Proceedings of the second ICF coaching research symposium* (pp. 69–78). International Coach Federation.

Edwards, J. L., & Green, K. (1997). *The effects of Cognitive Coaching on teacher efficacy and empowerment* [Unpublished manuscript]. School of Educational Leadership and Change, Fielding Graduate University.

Edwards, J. L., & Green, K. (1999a, April). *Growth in coaching skills over a three-year period: Progress toward mastery* [Paper presentation]. American Educational Research Association, Montreal, Quebec, Canada.

Edwards, J. L., & Green, K. (1999b, April). *Persisters versus nonpersisters: Characteristics of teachers who stay in a professional development program* [Paper presentation]. American Educational Research Association, Montreal, Quebec, Canada.

Edwards, J. L., Green, K., Lyons, C. A., Rogers, M. S., & Swords, M. (1998, April). *The effects of Cognitive Coaching and nonverbal classroom management on teacher efficacy and perceptions of school culture* [Paper presentation. American Educational Research Association, San Diego, CA, United States].

Edwards, J. L., & Newton, R. R. (1994a, February). *The effects of Cognitive Coaching on teacher efficacy and empowerment* [Unpublished manuscript]. School of Educational Leadership and Change, Fielding Graduate University.

Edwards, J. L., & Newton, R. R. (1994b, July). *The effects of Cognitive Coaching on teacher efficacy and thinking about teaching* [Unpublished manuscript]. School of Educational Leadership and Change, Fielding Graduate University.

Edwards, J. L., & Newton, R. R. (1995, April). *The effects of Cognitive Coaching on teacher efficacy and empowerment* [Paper presentation]. American Educational Research Association, San Francisco, CA, United States.

Eger, K. A. (2006). *Teachers' perception of the impact of Cognitive Coaching on their teacher thinking and behaviors* (Publication No. 3223584) [Doctoral dissertation, University of Illinois at Urbana-Champaign]. ProQuest Dissertations and Theses Global.

Ellison, J. (2003). Coaching principals for increased resourcefulness. In J. Ellison & C. Hayes (Eds.), *Cognitive Coaching^{SM}: Weaving threads of learning and change into the culture of an organization* (pp. 13–25). Christopher-Gordon.

Foster, N. (1989). *The impact of Cognitive Coaching on teachers' thought processes as perceived by cognitively coached teachers in the Plymouth-Canton Community School District* (Publication No. 8923848) [Doctoral dissertation, Michigan State University]. ProQuest Dissertations and Theses.

Freeman-Mack, N. M. (2020). *Examining fidelity in the implementation of instructional coaching* (Publication No. 27955875) [Doctoral dissertation, Manhattanville College]. ProQuest Dissertations and Theses Global.

Garmston, R., & Hyerle, D. (1988, August). *Professor's peer coaching program: Report on a 1987-88 pilot project to develop and test a staff development model for improving instruction at California State University* [Unpublished manuscript]. California State University at Sacramento.

Göker, S. D. (2020). Cognitive Coaching: A powerful supervisory tool to increase teacher sense of efficacy and shape teacher identity. *Teacher Development: An International Journal of Teachers' Professional Development, 24*(4), 559–582. https://doi.org/10.1080/13664530.2020.1791241

Göker, S. D., & Göker, M. U. (2021). Cognitive Coaching: Developing teachers of English as self-directed learners. *The Journal of Asia TEFL, 18*(3), 875–890. http://dx.doi.org/10.18823/asiatefl.2021.18.3.8.875

Gomez, R. L. (2005). *Cognitive Coaching: Bringing the ivory tower into the classroom* (Publication No. 3194204) [Doctoral dissertation, The University of North Carolina at Charlotte]. ProQuest Dissertations and Theses Global.

González, L. J. (2009). Los cinco estados de la mente en el counseling espiritual [Doctoral dissertation. Universidad Iberoamericana, México, D. F.]. http://www.uia.mx/

González Del Castillo, A. (2015). *Cognitive Coaching as a form of professional development in a linguistically diverse school* (Publication No. 3705178) [Doctoral dissertation, University of Missouri—Saint Louis]. ProQuest Dissertations and Theses Global.

Grochocki, J. (2018). *National board certification and Cognitive Coaching* (Publication No. 10751373) [Doctoral dissertation, Northern Arizona University]. ProQuest Dissertations and Theses Global.

Hall, G. E., & Hord, S. M. (2001). *Implementing change: Patterns, principles, and potholes*. Allyn and Bacon.

Hughes, A. J., & Partida, E. (2020). Promoting preservice STEM education teachers' metacognitive awareness: Professional development designed to improve teacher metacognitive awareness. *Journal of Technology Education, 32*(1), 5–20. http://doi.org/10.21061/jte.v32i1.a.1

Hunter, C. (2023). *The impact of Cognitive Coaching on high school English teachers' implementation of metacognitive reading strategies* (Publication No. 2878228811) [Doctoral dissertation, University of South Carolina]. ProQuest Dissertations and Theses Global.

Irons, N. A. (2014). *Coaching for questioning: A study on the impact of questioning* [Unpublished Capstone Action Research Project]. Fielding Graduate University, Santa Barbara, CA.

Jaede, M., Brosnan, P., Leigh, K., & Stroot, S. (2014, April). *Teaching to transgress: How Cognitive Coaching^{SM} influences the apprenticeship model in pre-service urban teacher education.* [Paper presentation]. American Educational Research Association, Philadelphia, PA. United States.

Johnson, J. B. (1997). *An exploratory study of teachers' efforts to implement Cognitive Coaching as a form of professional development: Waiting for Godot* (Publication No. 9729048) [Doctoral dissertation, University of St. Thomas (Minnesota)]. ProQuest Dissertations and Theses Global.

Joyce, B., & Showers, B. (2002). *Student achievement through staff development* (3rd ed.). ASCD.

Kilver, C. L. (2017). *The impact of student teaching on the preservice teacher* (Publication No. 10249793) [Doctoral dissertation, Western Illinois University]. ProQuest Dissertations and Theses Global.

Krpan, M. M. (1997). *Cognitive Coaching and efficacy, growth, and change for second-, third-, and fourth-year elementary school educators* (Publication No. 1384152) (Master's thesis). [Doctoral dissertation. California State University, Fullerton]. ProQuest Dissertations and Theses Global.

Lane, A. (2016). *Blended coaching to support administrator induction* (Publication No. 10150040) [Masters thesis, Saint Mary's College of California]. ProQuest Dissertations and Theses Global.

Liebmann, R. (1993). *Perceptions of human resource developers from product and service organizations as to the current and desired states of holonomy of managerial and manual employers* (Publication No. 9327374) [Doctoral dissertation, Seton Hall University]. ProQuest Dissertations and Theses Global.

Lim, L. (2016). *Understanding and negotiating the secondary vice-principal role: Perspectives of secondary principals* (Publication No. 4039) [Doctoral dissertation, The University of Western Ontario]. Electronic Thesis and Dissertation Repository.

Lindle, J. C. (2016). Posing questions for leadership development and practice: A coaching strategy for veteran school leaders. *International Journal of Leadership in Education: Theory and Practice, 19*(4), 438–463. http://dx.doi.org/10.1080/13603124.2015.1041555

MacGinitie, W. H., MacGinitie, R. K., Maria, K., & Dryer, L. G. (2000). *Gates-MacGinitie reading tests: Manual for scoring and interpretation* (4th ed.). Riverside.

Mackenzie, S. (2017). *Swimming in education reform policy currents: Cognitive Coach identities in Australian school contexts* [Unpublished master's thesis]. Charles Darwin University, Darwin, Northern Territory, Australia.

McLymont, E. F. (2000). *Mediated learning through the coaching approach facilitated by Cognitive Coaching* (Publication No. NQ59634) [Doctoral dissertation, University of Alberta (Canada)]. ProQuest Dissertations and Theses Global.

McLymont, E. F., & da Costa, J. L. (1998, April). *Cognitive Coaching: The vehicle for professional development and teacher collaboration* [Paper presentation]. American Educational Research Association, San Diego, CA, United States.

Moche, R. (1999). *Cognitive Coaching and reflective thinking of Jewish day school teachers* (Publication No. 9919383) [Doctoral dissertation, Yeshiva University]. ProQuest Dissertations and Theses Global.

Moche, R. (2000). Coaching teachers' thinking. *Journal of Jewish Education, 66*(3), 19–29. doi.org/10.1080/0021624000660304

Netolicky, D. M. (2016a). Coaching for professional growth in one Australian school: "Oil in water." *International Journal of Mentoring and Coaching in Education, 5*(2), 66–86.

Netolicky, D. M. (2016b). *Down the rabbit hole: Professional identities, professional learning, and change in one Australian school* [Unpublished doctoral dissertation]. Murdoch University, Murdoch, Australia.

Pavlock, K. C. (2023). *Getting to the heart of leading as a Cognitive Coach* (UMI No. 2821518038) [Doctoral dissertation, Eastern Michigan University]. ProQuest Dissertations and Theses Global.

Peery, S. D. (2022). *A qualitative case study of a midwestern district examining administrator and teacher perceptions of the impact of Cognitive Coaching on teaching performance* (Publication No. 29060794) [Doctoral dissertation, Evangel University]. ProQuest Dissertations and Theses Global.

Reed, L. A. (2007). *Case study of the implementation of Cognitive Coaching by an instructional coach in a Title I elementary school* (Publication No. 3270804) [Doctoral dissertation, Texas A&M University]. ProQuest Dissertations and Theses Global.

Rennick, L. W. (2002). *The relationship between staff development in balanced literacy instruction for kindergarten teachers and student literacy achievement* (Publication No. 3051831) [Doctoral dissertation, Saint Louis University]. ProQuest Dissertations and Theses Global.

Robinson, J. M. (2011). *Supporting National board candidates via Cognitive Coaching^{SM} conversations and communities of practice* (Publication No. 3449849) [Doctoral dissertation, Arizona State University]. ProQuest Dissertations and Theses Global.

Rogers, W. T. Hauserman, C. P., & Skytt, J. (2016). Using Cognitive Coaching to build school leadership capacity: A case study in Alberta. *Canadian Journal of Education, 39*(3), 1–29.

Sándigo, A. M. (2017). *Coaching tutors in academic English to improve tutoring for Hispanic students in higher education* (Publication No. 10687611) [Doctoral dissertation, Northern Arizona University]. ProQuest Dissertations and Theses Global.

Saphier, J. (1989). *The School Culture Survey*. Research for Better Teaching.

Schlosser, J. L. (1998). *The impact of Cognitive Coaching on the thinking processes of elementary school teachers* (Publication No. 9821080) [Doctoral dissertation, Brigham Young University]. ProQuest Dissertations and Theses Global.

Schraw, G., & Dennison, R. S. (1994). Assessing metacognitive awareness. *Contemporary Educational Psychology, 19*(4), 460–475. https://doi.org/10.1006/ceps.1994.1033

Skytt, J. K., Hauserman, C. P., Rogers, W. T., & Johnson, J. B. (2014). *Cognitive Coaching: Building school leadership capacity in Alberta's education system Leader2 Leader Project (L2L)*. Program report. The Alberta Teachers' Association.

Slinger, J. L. (2004). *Cognitive Coaching: Impact on students and influence on teachers* (Publication No. 3138974) [Doctoral dissertation, University of Denver]. ProQuest Dissertations and Theses Global.

Smith, M. C. (1997). *Self-reflection as a means of increasing teacher efficacy through Cognitive Coaching* (Publication No. 1384304) [Master's thesis, California State University, Fullerton]. ProQuest Dissertations and Theses Global.

Sparks-Langer, G. M., Simmons, J. M., Pasch, M., Colton, A., & Starko, A. (1990). Reflective pedagogical thinking: How can we promote it and measure it? *Journal of Teacher Education, 41*(5), 23–32. doi.org/10.1177/002248719004100504

Tennison, R. (2015). *A qualitative study of the factors supporting the implementation and sustainability of a deeply embedded Cognitive Coaching school culture* (Publication No. 10098660) [Doctoral dissertation, Southwest Baptist University]. ProQuest Dissertations and Theses Global.

Thinking Collaborative. (2022). *Cognitive Coaching seminars: Foundation training* (12th ed.). Thinking Collaborative.

Tschannen-Moran, M., & Gareis, C. R. (2004). *Principal sense of self-efficacy scale.* http://mxtsch.people.wm.edu/ResearchTools/PSE_OMR.pdf

Tschannen-Moran, M., & Hoy, A. W. (2001). Teacher efficacy: Capturing an elusive construct. *Teaching and Teacher Education, 17*(7), 783–805.

Ushijima, T. M. (1996). *Five states of mind scale for Cognitive Coaching: A measurement study* (Publication No. 9720306) [Doctoral dissertation, University of Southern California]. ProQuest Dissertations and Theses Global.

Uzat, S. L. (1999). *The relationship of Cognitive Coaching to years of teaching experience and to teacher reflective thought* (Publication No. 9947709) [Doctoral dissertation, The University of Southern Mississippi]. ProQuest Dissertations and Theses Global.

Walczak, B. (2022). *Using Cognitive Coaching to facilitate instructional reflection* (Publication No. 29255553) [Master's thesis, Rowan University]. ProQuest Dissertations and Theses Global.

Weatherford, D., & Weatherford, N. (1991). *Professional growth through peer coaching: A handbook for implementation* (Unpublished master's thesis). California State University, Sacramento, CA.

Wilcoxen, C., Bell, J., & Steiner, A. (2020). Empowerment through induction: Supporting the well-being of beginning teachers. *International Journal of Mentoring and Coaching in Education, 9*(1), 52–70. https://doi.org/10.1108/IJMCE-02-2019-0022

Wooten Burnett, S. W. (2014). *Cognitive Coaching℠: The impact on teacher candidates' teacher efficacy* [Doctoral dissertation, University of Louisville]. Electronic Theses and Dissertations, Paper 181.

Young, J. R. (1989). *Pre-service teachers' written reflection: The effect of structured training on pedagogical thinking* [Unpublished master's thesis]. Brigham Young University, Provo, Utah.

Philogelos
Something We Left Out

2

I'm struck by how laughter connects you with people. It's almost impossible to maintain any kind of distance or any sense of social hierarchy when you're just howling with laughter. Laughter is a force for democracy.

—John Cleese, comedian, actor, and producer

"Humor" means "fluid" or "moisture" in Latin. In archaic medical history, it was believed that the human body's four main fluids influenced a person's temperament. Today, however, humor defines our ability to feel our funny bone being tickled, to appreciate, engage in, and create laughter. It involves our ability to find joy, incongruity, or amusement in life's idiosyncratic situations.

"Philogelos" is the Greek word for lovers of laughter and humor. When we first wrote about Cognitive Coaching, we did not know the power of humor. But today, we realize that humor is an essential component in building trust and positive relationships among others and within groups.

Air traffic controllers, first responders, emergency-room medics, and teachers hold some of the world's most stressful professions. While cognitive coaches work to engage the highest level of executive functioning and creativity of their colleagues, stress may interfere with cognition, attention, learning, and memory (Abrams, 60, 61). When we are emotionally upset, we tend to underperform. Conversely, when we are calm, attuned, and open, we're more likely to achieve high performance.

Effective coaches, therefore, create a safe atmosphere of trust, collegiality, and joy. When coaches first meet their colleagues, and in subsequent conversations, colleagues may not know what to expect—will I be evaluated, criticized, advised? They may not know what roles they should play—follower, recipient, defendant, or thinking partner? Such uncertainty creates even additional stress.

At least three opportunities exist for bringing levity to a coaching conversation, one immediate, the other before the formal interaction. John Dyer, one of the first cognitive coaches from Canada, was known to be a funny man. John saw openings for humor everywhere. It's reported that he was seen at an intersection, waiting for a green light, pounding his fist on the dashboard and laughing so intensely that tears were running down his face. This was John, refining a funny story to use later that day. We wonder what the occupants of other cars thought was happening.

When colleagues encounter you against a backdrop of humor, they may be at ease immediately on meeting. If you are anything like John, they may relax at first encounter, in unconscious anticipation of friendly interchange. A third option is to begin your conferences with a funny story, an embarrassing situation you experienced, something funny about a student comment, or remembrance from your past that brought laughter and smiles. If you have proximity to preschool kids, the laughter possibilities are endless.

There is a link between humor and psychological safety. Even the anticipation of laughing has been shown to decrease cortisol (our stress hormone) and epinephrine (our fight-or-flight hormone), making us feel safer, calmer, and less stressed. And when we're less stressed, we do better work.

Laughter does more than make one feel good. Laughter alters brain functioning and boosts production of dopamine, a neurotransmitter associated with the brain's reward and "feel good" system. It reduces cortisol, the brain's stress hormone, and may even improve memory. Laughter triggers the release of oxytocin, often referred to as the trust hormone because of the way it prompts our brain to create emotional bonds. Laughter quickens the path to candor and vulnerability. Shared laughter doesn't just create closeness in the moment—it's equally effective at strengthening relationships over time.

> Creativity is intelligence having fun. (Einstein)

Stress experienced by teachers also trickles down to students. Luckily, so does their joy. Comedy writer Doug Hall suggests that brain power can be increased three- to five-fold simply by laughing and having fun before working on a problem. We know that in our adult interactions, something funny will break us up, and momentarily exhausted and refreshed, we rebegin our work. Humor also helps us remember. By flooding our reward center with the neurotransmitter dopamine, humor engenders deeper levels of focus and long-term retention. Using humor makes your content more engaging in the moment and more memorable after the session. Humor also ignites the creativity center of our brains.

Stanford University researcher Jennifer Aaker (Aaker & Bagdonas, 2021) describes the science behind laughter and trust:

> Shared laughter accelerates trust. Even reminiscing about moments of shared laughter makes individuals report being 23% more satisfied in their relationships. Research by Gallup shows that one of the greatest drivers of employee performance is having a close friend at work—employees who work in high-trust environments are 32 times more likely to take risks that might benefit their company, 11 times more likely to see higher levels of innovation and six times more likely to achieve higher levels of performance. (Kettner, 2023).

Naomi Bagdonas (Stanford Graduate School of Business) says, "Laughing makes us more creative, bonded and resilient. Humor is an elixir for *trust* and an antidote to arrogance."

And, James J. Walsh, M.D. (1928), long ago found that people who laugh actually live longer than those who don't laugh. Few people realize that health actually varies according to the amount of laughter they experience. (How old are *you*, so far?)

Can we learn to engage humor? Learning to be more humorous, humble, and humane is a valuable endeavor that can greatly enhance your personal growth and interactions with others. Here are some suggestions on how to develop these traits:

- Have a positive attitude toward learning. Encourage your colleagues to laugh and have fun while working on projects or doing group work.
- Make a point of telling jokes and funny stories during coaching conversations.
- Search for opportunities with your colleagues to find humor and to laugh. If they cannot find such opportunities, laugh anyway.
- While it may be difficult to find reasons for laughter, it's easy to simply laugh—laugh on credit—that's almost as good as genuine laughter.
- Invite your colleague to share humorous stories, bring in jokes and cartoons. Discuss what makes a situation humorous.
- As a coach, laugh at yourself in the presence of your colleagues. Modeling is one of the most powerful learning strategies.

Table 2.1

	Smiles	Chuckles	Belly-laugh	Hilarity
Coach				
Coachee				

How do we know we're getting better at finding humor?

- Expose yourself to comedy: watch stand-up shows, comedy movies, and comedians on TV to understand different comedic styles and learn the art of timing, delivery, and wit.
- Read humorous literature: explore books, articles, and blogs by funny authors to gain inspiration and expand your sense of humor.
- Practice observation and wordplay: pay attention to your surroundings and find humor in everyday situations. Experiment with puns, wordplay, and clever observation.
- Rate your humor quotient: reflect on a conference with a colleague, and check your humor level. Start with a smile, graduate to a chuckle, progress to a belly-laugh, and strive towards hysterical.

CAUTION: THERE'S A MUDDY ROAD AHEAD! Though we shouldn't need to point this out, never be vulgar or use humor to belittle, disparage, or demean other individuals, races, genders, religions, or ethnicities.

References

Aaker, J., & Bagdonas, N. (2021). *Humour, seriously: Why humour is a superpower at work and in life*. Penguin Business.

Kettner, G. (2023, February 3). Building trust with laughter. *WorkHappy™*.

Walsh, J. J. (1928). *Laughter and health*. D. Appleton and Company.

Section II

Relevance in an Emerging World

Introduction

Cultures that don't continue to learn and adapt, of course, do not survive or at best limp along in less than effective states. This is true in both the animal kingdom and human enterprises. After eighty years of Dutch colonization in the Indian Ocean, the dodo bird disappeared, unable to adapt to a rapidly changing environment.

Cultures committed to continuing learning provide mechanisms for employees and managers to increase personal and collective skills and knowledge. They epitomize traditions of continuing refinement and respect for members of the organization. Their programs for continuing learning employ, in addition to other approaches, lectures, reading, discussion groups, conferences, and classes. This dedication to continuous learning often includes coaching.

For example, nurses who fail to continue to learn fall behind innovations or new hospital procedures. Self-assurance and effectiveness most likely decline as does quality of patient care, and often trust from the families they serve, perhaps leading to cultures of resignedness. During the Covid-19 pandemic, hospitals and staff were tested beyond human capacity, yet because of the determined commitment to caring for their patients, health care employees continually gave—even to the point of personally declining health and resources.

Cultures committed to continuing learning provide mechanisms for employees and managers to increase personal and collective skills and knowledge. They epitomize traditions of continuing refinement and respect for members of the organization. Their programs for continuing learning employ, in addition to other approaches, lectures, reading, discussion groups, conferences, and classes. Their dedication to continuous learning often includes coaching.

An example of this is found in WakeMed Canadian Health Services in which doctors, nurses and administrators received training in Cognitive Coaching. Some quotes:

> Cognitive Coaching is a method of listening effectively and empowering an individual to reach insightful and intuitive decisions concerning challenges they are faced with.
>
> The colleague that wanted opinion and advice, instead of offering advice I put some of the skills I had learned in Cognitive Coaching into play. I was able to listen in a different way. By pausing and paraphrasing I was able to clarify for the colleague a really great solution on her own and one that I wouldn't have been able to come up with.

> The patient who was struggling with a screening recommendation. Prior to this training I would have reiterated the need for the screening. It turns out that this patient was afraid of needles so [paraphrased] she wanted to feel safe but also wanted to get this done. In the end. The patient felt heard and ended up taking the screening. I felt more satisfied with this interaction. Hospital administrators recommended that "We incorporate this style of communication in everything we do." It would be important for us to deal with people as people . . . putting their needs first . . . and create a safe place to offer our expertise.

Business and industries unrelated to public or private schools assign value, as do we, to coaching programs for employees. Coaching is not reserved for just small organizations but indeed is practiced in companies with over 20,000 people in the workforce. One of these enterprises is the International Trade Association (ITA) whose employees work in over seventy countries.

Earlier, owner and then codirectors of the Center for Thinking Collaborative, Carolee Hayes and Carol Simoneau collaborated with Margie Sills-Maerov to develop a pilot coaching program for Health Care in Canada. Two Thinking Collaborative training associates, John Clarke and John Dyer, conducted CC training for medical staff and began developing individual trainers to teach CC within the health industry.

About this time other trainers, including ourselves, were field testing portions of the CC curriculum with the US Air Force, Sacramento County Probation Officers, a Sacramento marketing firm, and the World Health Center at the UN in Copenhagen. Father Luís continues to teach his parishioners and clergy Cognitive Coaching, first in Rome and now in Mexico.

The goal of learning Cognitive Coaching is to develop the capacities and identity of colleagues as mediators, who can in turn help to develop the capacities for self-directedness in others. An ultimate goal in Cognitive Coaching is autonomy and the capacity for holonomic living.

Cognitive Reflection and Neurodiversity

Diana Rosberg and Bridget McNamer

Definitions and Foundational Understandings (p. 38)

Natural Cognitive Awareness and Adaptation (p. 38)

Alignment with Cognitive Coaching Approaches (p. 39)

A Third Option: Distributed Cognitive Coaching (p. 40)

Conscious Application of Introspection and Cognitive Coaching Approaches (p. 41)

Expanding the Conversation: Neurodiverse Leaders Driving Change (p. 43)

Conclusion: A Call to Action (p. 43)

Picture this: a colleague on your leadership team displays keen gifts—perhaps an aptitude for analyzing and making sense of complex patterns, enhanced sensitivity toward people, or an ability to identify creative out-of-the-box solutions—all of which benefit your team's collective efficacy. At the same time, you've noticed that they tend to withdraw after a burst of productive activity, may struggle with ordinary small talk or team engagements, or display facial or physical tics in moments of heightened stress.

Chances are your colleague may possess a neurodivergent brain.

When we hear the term "neurodivergent," we immediately think of students diagnosed with autism, dyslexia, or attention deficit hyperactivity disorder (ADHD). What we generally *don't* imagine is those students, grown up, working alongside us as colleagues. And what we *rarely* consider are the strategies these individuals develop to navigate workplaces and societies not set up with their neurosignatures in mind-strategies that align closely with Cognitive Coaching principles.

This chapter shines a light on how neurodivergent individuals use self-awareness, problem-solving, and reflection—all associated with Cognitive Coaching—to navigate a world built for neurotypicals. It explores how a convergence of neurodiversity appreciation and Cognitive Coaching practices can help teams thrive.

Definitions and Foundational Understandings

- *Neurotypical:* a person whose brain operates and processes information in typical ways
- *Neurodivergent:* a person whose brain operates and/or processes information in atypical ways. Divergences vary in impact, ranging from challenging to highly advantageous depending on context and individual neurosignature
- *Neurosignature:* each brain's unique way of operating and processing information. Like fingerprints, we all have one

Neurodivergent individuals often develop strategies to navigate neurotypical systems and norms, such as:

- *Masking and mimicking:* adopting learned behaviors to integrate into neurotypical communities
- *Understanding neurotypical models:* analyzing neurotypical behavior to adapt more effectively
- *Metacognition:* gaining deeper awareness of personal strengths, challenges, and problem-solving styles
- *Advocacy:* learning to articulate and advocate for personal needs

These strategies, tailored to each individual, mirror the journey of Cognitive Coaching: reflection, self-directed growth, and problem-solving.

Natural Cognitive Awareness and Adaptation

Eryn Sherman is a talented curriculum coordinator with bipolar disorder. She consciously monitors fluctuations in her mood and energy levels, and considers how those levels influence the work of her colleagues, so that she can better collaborate with her teams. Though she has never undertaken Cognitive Coaching, Eryn leverages introspection and metacognition to navigate her work effectively.

Leaders like Eryn demonstrate a unique cognitive awareness, honed through necessity. Neurodivergent individuals must navigate systems designed for neurotypicals, where unspoken norms and systems are intuitive for most. To bridge this gap, many neurodivergent individuals develop evolving models to monitor and adapt their behaviors, environments, and approaches, allowing them to see and do things differently than neurotypicals: more effectively, more efficiently, with greater attention to detail, or more creatively.

With limited scope for changing how society works, these models typically evolve into strategies for the neurodivergent individual to adapt their approach to specific situations. Observation leads to introspection and results in effective change; the cycle is self-reinforcing. All of this can be exhausting work, with incredible benefits to creativity, efficiency, and efficacy, for both neurodiverse individuals and the communities they serve.

For instance, those sensitive to sensory environments—such as many autists, highly sensitive persons (HSPs), and individuals with ADHD—often create systems to detect and mitigate sensory overload. Others develop systems to account for differences in how important information, events and tasks are typically signaled.

Neurodivergents leverage this introspection to solve complex problems. Richard Jaberzadeh, an educational technology systems specialist with dyslexia, recalls one instance where his school's leadership team was overwhelmed by new and conflicting demands on the schedule. By recognizing ineffective team interactions and harnessing his brain's capacity for pattern recognition, manipulation, and development, Richard developed a solution. This was only possible because his team understood his need for hyperfocus and distraction-free work—evidence of personal metacognition paired with collective support.

If such intentionality, already frequently observed in neurodiverse individuals, could be more broadly developed, it could be instrumental in unlocking the potential both of the leaders who undertake the challenge and of the workplaces that recognize neurodiverse inclusion as one necessary ingredient of highly successful teams.

Alignment with Cognitive Coaching Approaches

The reflection, metacognition, and self-directed growth espoused by Cognitive Coaching are obvious allies for neurodiverse individuals navigating a neurotypical world, and we have seen many examples of individuals using tools and strategies that could have been taken straight from Cognitive Coaching materials. In some cases, individuals heard about these methods from their coaches, whether these coaches were explicitly drawing from Cognitive Coaching training or not. Glenn Krancher is a coach for neurodivergent adults, based in the Netherlands. He has found that progress toward goals for his clientele starts with essential self-awareness. Most of his clients come to him with negative self-perceptions. Through initial coaching aimed at raising their recognition of their strengths and skills, he helps them gain a more positive self-image. Further coaching helps them better understand how their conditions present as, or come up against, obstacles in a neurotypical setting. This then leads to coaching around problem-solving, including a combination of tools, workarounds, and self-advocacy.

The coauthor of this chapter, Bridget McNamer, is a coach for women leaders in schools, some of them also neurodivergents. She, too, has found that progress toward goals for her clientele closely follows the protocols espoused by Cognitive Coaching. Self-awareness is the baseline. Clients may initially come to her eager to plunge forward into a system (school leadership) not created with them in mind, leaving them frustrated by obstacles and plagued by self-doubt—a scenario that mimics what neurodivergents encounter. Early coaching involves grounding these leaders in appreciation for their particular strengths, attributes, and a sense of purpose. It evolves to greater awareness of how these factors may come up against resistance in a system designed primarily by and for men. Further coaching identifies a combination of courage, tools, and self-advocacy to effectively address this resistance. While not explicitly drawing on Cognitive Coaching principles, this arc of coaching echoes those principles closely.

A Third Option: Distributed Cognitive Coaching

Beyond natural cognitive awareness, and explicit coaching that parallels the Cognitive Coaching approach, a third option suggests itself: Is it possible that as Cognitive Coaching has spread over the years, it has provided touchpoints which are now embedded in multiple networks, and available to all of us?

Through the resources that neurodiverse individuals consult to better understand how their brains are wired, through the professionals who diagnose neurodivergent conditions and the coaches who provide support, and through the humorous TikToks which lovingly highlight and dissect neurodiverse experiences, has our interconnected world, fueled at least in part by social media and its ability to create communities of like-minded people dispersed around the world, spread the tools and strategies inherent in Cognitive Coaching so thoroughly that they are being employed by many who have no conscious knowledge of their origins?

Our interviewees are potent illustrations of such a phenomenon. Each of them, whether they have direct experience with Cognitive Coaching or not, uses language and applies strategies which are aligned with its core principles. It would be hard to explain this fully without considering the possibility that our interviewees, in their personal networks, are encountering resources which have been influenced by Cognitive Coaching's designs for planning, reflecting, and problem-resolving conversations.

Conscious Application of Introspection and Cognitive Coaching Approaches

Real-life stories illustrate what we've been seeing with self-directed growth, such as leaders who build personal systems for self-coaching, using cognitive awareness as a tool for problem-solving and development. Bengt Rosberg has been a school leader for over twenty-five years and is also an HSP. His strengths include the ease with which he makes emotional connections with colleagues, students, and family members, and his ability to empathize with their needs. By taking on their challenges as his own, he is better able to generate bespoke solutions. A tough side effect, though, is that his personal emotional load becomes heavier and heavier. To support his own needs, over the years he has used reflection and introspection to understand what sort of events will cause overload. From there, he uses planning to better prepare for situations that could be challenging, and to preemptively embed recovery experiences into his schedule, thereby reducing negative repercussions.

Other neurodiverse leaders carefully review past experiences, exploring actions and choices that didn't necessarily serve them well in the past, in order to identify better ways to handle new situations. Deb Lane, a seasoned educational leader and leadership development consultant, recalls her early struggles with dyslexia, in which she relied on diversions and compensations to combat the challenges she encountered in making sense of words. Through much training in self-awareness, including through Cognitive Coaching, Deb has developed adaptive strategies for information processing challenges and has also, indirectly, greatly heightened her emotional intelligence (EI). She prides herself on her ability to "read a room," employing emotional and neural sensitivities that she has honed over the years. This allows her to quickly build rapport and emotional connection with people in ways that have served her very well in her leadership roles.

Diana Rosberg is another veteran school leader and a coauthor of this chapter. She is autistic and embraces the many ways in which her autistic brain gives her a special perspective. Her specialties are wide-ranging and from the outside don't always seem to fit together: strategic planning, K-12 curriculum design, and personal finance coaching are three recurring themes. The common thread? They all require the development of simple-to-execute, multiyear, multistrand plans with meaningful goals. Many of her tools are straight from the stereotypical autism toybox: spreadsheets and personal to-do lists for a start. But she credits much of her success to approaches that she was given by Bob Garmston when he trained her in Adaptive Schools approaches. Through deep analysis of the goals she is trying to achieve (such as a shared vision for a high school teaching team or strands for a strategic plan that would reflect the input of multiple stakeholder groups), she is able to home in on what really matters and then select appropriate protocols to achieve the goals. Without the reflection and planning that Cognitive Coaching promotes, her work would be much harder and/or less effective.

It's also valuable to put intentional metacognition to use in team settings so that everyone benefits from collaborative efforts. One team we've worked with has two members who identify as neurodivergent; at their request, the team shared key information about their personal thinking and working styles, strengths, and blind spots (a sort of "user's manual," if you will). This explicit approach to mutual understanding leads to productive division of labor and quicker resolution of challenges. When any team member needs to design a process (for creating a product, for evaluating complex options, etc.), they immediately offer the initial work to their autistic colleague, who can typically rattle off a customized, simple, and usable structure within a few minutes. The team works together to take the process to the next level, rather than wasting time by having everyone participate in the initial design stage.

And when this same team faces any intractable problem that has the potential to stop work in its tracks—perhaps because it has presented in a black-and-white, yes-or-no dichotomy—that team knows to turn to their colleague with ADHD. As a creative thinker, skilled at seeing connections, patterns, and options that elude many others, this colleague is adept at rejecting the dichotomy and offering up a "sideways" solution that meets everyone's needs and keeps work flowing. The team has put significant effort into thinking about thinking, and recognizing what different brains have to offer, leading to efficiency and efficacy in their practices.

Expanding the Conversation: Neurodiverse Leaders Driving Change

Efforts like those described above have enormous potential to create ripple effects within their organizations. When cognitive awareness is put to effective use, leading to growth for individuals and teams, it can, quite naturally, cause everyone involved to take notice of benefits and to lean into what's working. People who have engaged in this sort of productive collaboration often seek to expand on their experiences. Individuals look for clues as to what's working, and apply, as best they can, those strategies in new contexts. In this paradigm, once inclusion increases success, that leads to further inclusive practices.

When neurodiverse leaders use coaching and introspection to embrace their strengths, they challenge outdated notions of what leadership "should" look like. They model inclusive practices and create ripple effects in their schools and organizations. For example, we know of several hiring committees who now provide at least some of their interview questions to applicants ahead of time, reducing anxiety, which can be particularly stressful for neurodivergent applicants, and allowing for the kind of thought-through answers that truly show the interviewee's skill set. This practice, and others like it, supports the building of truly balanced and inclusive workplaces.

Organizations also benefit from actively providing coaching to their employees, whether neurodivergent or neurotypical. Cognitive Coaching, employed widely, empowers individuals to amplify their contributions and encourages organizations to reconsider how well traditional systems are meeting their needs.

Neurodiverse individuals are perhaps uniquely positioned to propel this type of inclusive organizational growth. With natural tendencies for introspection and problem-solving, supported by explicit coaching, they can serve as models and leaders for the development of strategies to build inclusive, productive teams, and model a new paradigm for leadership: one that values diversity and fosters growth. We encourage all employers to invite their neurodivergent colleagues to join and lead meaningful conversations about how best to move forward.

Conclusion: A Call to Action

The stories and strategies shared in this chapter highlight the transformative potential of neurodiverse leaders who embrace cognitive awareness and coaching principles. We encourage schools to:

- recognize and celebrate neurodiverse strengths at *all* levels, including in leadership teams
- provide coaching opportunities for all employees, neurodivergent and neurotypical alike
- foster inclusive practices that raise awareness and empower individuals and teams.

By doing so, we can unlock the full potential of neurodiversity—not just for individuals but for the leadership teams, their organizations, and the communities they serve.

Developing Leaders' Efficacy . . . Virtually

Kendall Zoller and Michael Tonkin

4

The Kickoff (p. 46)

Vulnerability (p. 47)

Engagement (p. 48)

How Do We Do That? (p. 49)

Relationships (p. 50)

Two Final Thoughts on Relationships (p. 51)

> In organizations, real power and energy is generated through relationships. The pattern of relationships and the capacities to form them are more important than tasks, functions, roles and positions.
> —Margaret Wheatley

This chapter paints a picture of how a leader's efficacy is strengthened by deepened confidence and competence through a twelve-hour virtual class on storytelling. The storytelling training is for middle and senior leaders in a global organization. Over the past four years, over one hundred and twenty sessions have been delivered to over 1,600 participants from over seventy countries, representing many languages and cultures. Although the participants are from the same organization, their offices are geographically located in different countries, so not everyone knows each other. The culture of this global company is rooted in a century-long practice of storytelling, and it is embedded in their culture. Those attending range from five to thirty years of experience in leadership. They lead groups from fifty into the hundreds in manufacturing, packaging, shipping, marketing, finance, legal, and product development.

We begin by sharing how the kickoff session is delivered to frame how the learning environment creates a space for vulnerability in an engaging design that develops relationships and trust, resulting in personal efficacy by enhancing confidence and competence.

The Kickoff

We begin our story with one class in their Southeast Asian market. As the start time approaches in our one-hour virtual kickoff, participants begin to log on. The host client delivers a brief introduction and framing of the course. The participants are from Indonesia, Malaysia, Taiwan, Japan, and Fiji. When the guest speaker finishes, the two facilitators welcome each participant in English.

The kickoff begins with the lead facilitator sharing a story that is personal and revealing in that it brings to light his own self-imposed limitations, fears, and anxieties. He opens with "My first book was released in 2010. And that was a challenge, although the challenge did not end there. No, it continues, lurking in the dark recesses of my own self-imposed limits. It is the challenge of doubt, the challenge of a masquerade, the grand imposter . . ."

The twelve participants, strangers to each other, listen and after the story they are invited to share their name, what they do for the organization, and how they feel about being here. At the conclusion of the introductions, the program and prework are introduced, and they adjourn, knowing in two weeks they will meet again for three consecutive three-and-a-half-hour virtual days.

We share this scenario with you to illustrate the ways the structure of the virtual experience builds efficacy by creating a learning environment where vulnerability thrives and relationships develop.

Our thesis addresses the following: To what extent can a virtual training enhance the efficacy of participants by building their confidence? We share this story with you by explaining how a virtual storytelling program opens space to be vulnerable and engaged in meaningful ways that build relationships. The result is newfound confidence and competence in leaders' efficacy when storytelling.

Vulnerability

In this context, *vulnerability* is the openness and willingness of individuals to expose their true selves, including their weaknesses, uncertainties, and emotions, in a work environment. Components of vulnerability include authenticity, trust, transparency, empathy, compassion, and collaboration.

From the onset in the kickoff, vulnerability is modeled by the opening story. The facilitator reveals some personal qualities that he is not necessarily proud of, yet they are ever-present qualities that cast shadows on life. Vulnerability is again modeled by the facilitators when they begin introductions; they go first and share both professional and personal contexts about what they do as well as how they feel about being here.

The intentional modeling of vulnerability by the facilitators contributes to creating a space where participants are encouraged to be emotionally and cognitively vulnerable if they choose to do so. At the kickoff, participants are asked to come to the next session with a story ready to share with the group during the first module.

In the minds of the facilitators, their consciousness is high in that they are "thinking about [the] work in the moment and being willing to be aware of [their] own actions" (Costa & Garmston, 2013, p. 27) as they facilitate the kickoff. For instance, as participants log on, the two facilitators briefly welcome participants so as to position the guest speaker. They maintain the importance of modeling vulnerability in the opening story while being mindful of their interactions to model relationship-building as well.

When the first three-and-a-half-hour workshop begins, participants experience three opportunities for vulnerability in the first hour. First, the group engages in a community-building activity where they are asked to share something from the heart. The facilitators might say something along the lines of "Share a gift your family or friends say you have." The facilitators model first, then the group goes into a breakout group as a trio for a few minutes.

The second opportunity for vulnerability is not an experience but an anticipatory frame. This frame creates the spaces for participants to be public in their learning and to begin to balance their individual tensions between authenticity, competence, and confidence. This is accomplished by referencing the four levels of learning that include unconscious incompetence, conscious incompetence, conscious competence, and unconscious competence.

To anchor the impact of the anticipatory frame, the facilitator's final statement from this visual representation of the levels of learning is "Our hope is that each of you experience all four levels of learning in our time together."

The third opportunity for experiencing vulnerability is when participants share their stories for the first time. To lead participants into breakout groups, a slide shows the visual exit directions for giving peer feedback. Within the text of the exit directions, we ask participants to dip their toes into the bath of vulnerability by providing prompts that focus on content, not delivery; and on what they enjoyed, not what was boring. These prompts also do not ask participants to comment on anything they have not yet learned from the course content.

The prompts are:

1. What connected with me in your story was . . . (choices, feelings, images, etc.)
2. The details or moments in your story that I enjoyed and would like to hear more about were . . .
3. The gaps in your story that I would like to know more about were . . .

They disappear into their breakout groups, and fate is cast to the wind with the hope they will stay on task. This is not the only 25-minute breakout over the program; in fact, participants have five more opportunities to share their same story across the whole program. Participants are provided with the rationale behind this design, which intends to reduce the cognitive load of having to come up with a new story each time. By explicitly sharing this intention with participants, they are able to fully commit to learning new skills and techniques.

Being in these small breakout groups with new members each time creates a safe space for participants to share, engage with each other in new ways, and be authentic in their presence. It is this space that serves as a place for vulnerability and learning, allowing them to reveal their storytelling skills and begin the journey of developing their confidence and competence.

Engagement

Virtually, *engagement* is when participants are active and involved with each other during whole group and breakout situations. Participants are focused on the topic and each other, collaborative in their learning, and have a sense of belonging in the virtual community.

We know these breakouts are not an engagement strategy on their own because sending disengaged learners to a 25-minute breakout spells disaster. When it comes to engagement, our jobs as facilitators are to create the right conditions when we're all together. Setting the stage for learners to be present and emails to be parked so that learners can connect the dots between the training experience and applying it immediately to work.

How Do We Do That?

One way is the interactions of the second facilitator. Rather than compete for equal airtime or play the role of back-end virtual administrator, the second facilitator has a major role in engaging the audience. Using the virtual chat function, Facilitator #2 might comment, "Listen for the structure in his story . . .", "Did you hear that paraphrase?", or even, "His favourite word filler is 'and.'" These all help to keep learners on the edge of their seats and engaged. The interactions between facilitators are an example of their interdependence and efficacy.

The facilitators' interdependence is always focused on the common good toward supporting a positive learning environment. They seek and model collegiality and draw on their collective resources as masters of their craft. The continuous seeking of engagement contributes to an environment where participants feel a sense of efficacy in their own learning.

The personal efficacy of the facilitators in their pursuit of learning creates a space for participants to also engage in public learning. An interdependence emerges among participants where individuals hold high expectations for themselves as well as their colleagues, and this increases their self-confidence.

We know that for learners to feel engaged, they need to learn, develop, and grow early on in the learning experience. To support this learning, one of our intentional moves in each workshop is to invite members of the group to receive one-on-one coaching with the lead facilitator in front of the whole group. The process for feedback starts with the lead facilitator and then moves to the audience where participants are invited to contribute.

> "Kormal, you heard Vivian's initial story in the morning of day one. What are some things you're noticing now?"
>
> Kormal says, "I like the change you made to the structure of the story. You nailed the gesture moves. I think you could have paused longer when you made your transition."

This coaching interaction has two impacts. On the coach, it builds their consciousness. From the coachee's perspective, it builds efficacy by enhancing their craftsmanship, and this leads to greater confidence and competence.

It is also important to mention that, in this program, one or two senior learners are invited to undertake coaching with the lead facilitator in front of the group on day one. By day three, that leader is invited to take on the role of lead coach. This approach keeps our senior cohort engaged, the more junior

Levels of Learning

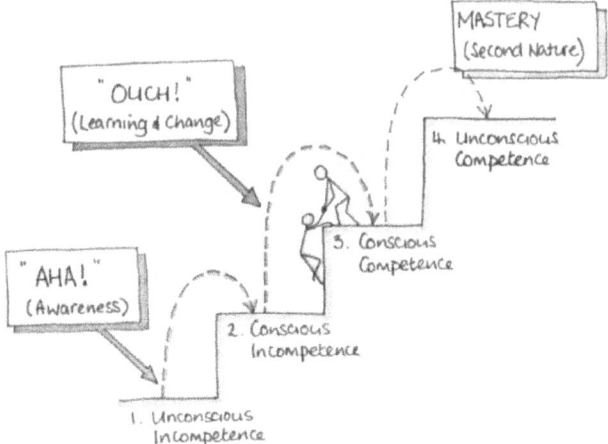

Figure 4.1 Levels of learning from management training programs (Martin M. Broadwell, February 1969)

cohort on their toes, while facilitators manage the process. It is also a positive symbol from facilitators that they are passing on the torch for participants to continue on without them, knowing that "they've got this."

For the remainder of the program, participants are requested to be specific with their peers on the feedback they wish to receive. Participants have the following instructions:

Before the story, the storyteller . . .

1. Tells others, "Please give me specific feedback on . . ."

After the story, others . . .

2. Provide feedback to you, based on your wishes.
3. Provide additional feedback outside of what was requested by you.

By having participants identify the specific feedback they wish to receive, hierarchies are broken down because more junior staff have permission to provide feedback. As a result, each individual's craftsmanship deepens and efficacy strengthens.

Relationships

In a virtual setting, *relationships* require intentional effort to develop and maintain. Relationships are at the foundation of quality learning. Engaging participants in novel and intentional protocols results in new associations with each other which serves as a catalyst for creativity and innovation.

Imagine the following scenario. It's day two and groups are returning from a lengthy breakout practice. The lead facilitator welcomes the group back to the plenary room and invites one person from each breakout to respond to the same question:

"What was that experience like for you and your group?"

Kelmond talks about the experience in a playful way and shares a funny anecdote about something that happened in his group. The facilitator says, "For you, it was more fun than work."

Shai's language changes from day one, moving from less "I" and more "we," and the facilitator adds, "So, for you, your group is making progress."

Rohan shares the challenge for him of being authentic and others in that same breakout group chime in with comments to support his own self-assessment. In response the facilitator shares with Rohan and the group members, "It's a challenge to mechanically implement the skills and to feel as though you are being authentic."

And finally, Samir says, "I have nothing to add!" The facilitator uses a voice of excitement and humor, saying, "So you got this!"—unsure if what Samir said was a cue that she is feeling good about herself or doesn't need to repeat what everyone else has just said. She responds, "Yeah!"

What is also important to mention is that with just about every participant comment, one of the facilitators offers a paraphrase. The influence of paraphrasing contributes to the participants feeling heard, understood, and safe in sharing their learning publicly. These casual engagements, intentional in design, support individuals that come together for the first time or between people with high internal familiarity.

Two Final Thoughts on Relationships

First, co-facilitators need to role-model their relationship with each other in front of the group, to set the tone for the experience. And this can build over time. To truly model this, co-facilitators need to move from content/process buddies to good mates that genuinely care for each other and hold a desire to make the other look good. The flexibility to organically navigate the development of this relationship is demonstrated by the facilitators' comfort with ambiguity, authentic sense of humor, and individual capacity to change their minds in a single moment as their interplay unfolds.

Second, it's a respect thing with the audience. The facilitators assimilate with their audiences in many ways, including pronouncing individuals' names in full (not nicknames) and calling out time by minutes to fit with the different time zones, that is, "If we could return from the breakout at fifteen to the hour." By using names correctly and acknowledging time the facilitators keep the focus on the relationships between them and the group.

As the final workshop draws to a close, the facilitators ask the group, "What is something you appreciated from the program? Who would like to go first?" Answers vary from group to group, and yet there is always a constant, the learning. On the learning front, the participants' comments tend to go something like "I liked how you structured the program. You gave us some theory, we then practiced with our peers and got feedback, and you then gave us time to reflect and make further improvements." And they're right. This is exactly what was done across multiple touchpoints in the program. Individuals gained confidence, efficacy, and craftsmanship knowing that "this stuff works."

A powerful example of the developing efficacy came from a participant from Fiji who has been in leadership for a couple of decades. At the kickoff we engaged in a conversation with him, and he said that we hoped we might offer something for him, knowing he comes from a culture rooted in storytelling. He laughed and said that he was looking forward to it. At the end of the training, while participants were sharing, he said, "In Fiji, our boats are very important to us. They provide the means to get food, support our families, and visit nearby communities. Without our boat, we would not survive. Let me share a saying we have in Fijian. In English it means, 'You helped me move my boat.' Thank you!"

References

Broadwell, M. M. (1969, February 20). Teaching for learning (XVI). *The Gospel Guardian*. Retrieved May 11, 2018, from wordsfitlyspoken.org

Costa, A., & Garmston, R. (2013). *Cognitive coaching seminars foundation training* (9th ed.). Cognitive Coaching Seminars.

Diversity Matters
Creating and Sustaining Systems of Belonging

Phil Echols, Stacie L. Stanley, and Delores B. Lindsey

5

Creating a Sense of Inclusion and Belonging (p. 54)
Creating Stronger Work Groups (p. 54)
Organization Culture, Diversity, and Belonging (p. 55)
Talking to One Another in a Diverse Workplace (p. 56)
Five Stages to Solving Complex Problems (p. 58)

To better understand the reasoning behind diversity, equity, and inclusion action plans for today's organizations, a walk back through history would help. In the late fall of 1960, six-year-old Ruby Bridges became the first African American to attend an all-white public school. As she entered William Frantz Elementary School, she was met with acts of racism, thrown objects, and crowds yelling racial slurs, and more. She was escorted by federal marshals to her kindergarten class. Barbara Henry, a 28-year-old white teacher, was the only educator willing to include Ruby in the classroom. Upon hearing Ruby's class assignment, families withdrew their children, leaving Ms. Henry with only Ruby in her classroom. Barbara taught Ruby as if she were an entire class.

Sixty years later, classrooms are integrated across the country. It started with an acknowledgment and belief that diversity and inclusion enrich the learning experiences of all students in the classroom. Ruby's story is one of personal courage and fortitude and of hopefulness while facing oppressive systems. In this example, the student, the teacher, and the supreme court that ruled in favor of school integration all placed a value on diversity and inclusion. This illustrates two reasons diversity is necessary: to create a sense of inclusiveness and to make stronger work groups.

Creating a Sense of Inclusion and Belonging

Valuing diversity means valuing our differences, experiences, background, heritage, and perspective that individuals bring to a group. When we aren't valuing, honoring, acknowledging, and leveraging diversity in the room, we're missing an opportunity for something greater, for a better product, and for a better outcome and results. When we aren't intentional about honoring diversity or leveraging diversity, we cultivate marginalization. When properly leveraged, the broader the spectrum of demographics, backgrounds, and perspectives, the more durable the team is in terms of teamwork and collaboration (Garmston & McKanders, 2022). Establishing a context of psychological safety means people feel valued, seen, heard, accepted, and included. Acknowledging and honoring diversity is the first step in creating a psychologically safe environment. Being intentional about valuing diversity by including the experiences, voices, and expertise of diverse people is the next step. By creating spaces of belonging, educators demonstrate that individuals are accepted, valued, and safe.

In the Act of Forgiveness, Lovingkindness, and Peace, Jack Kornfield shares that in the Babembe Tribe of Africa, when someone commits a crime or wrongdoing, the tribal members circle around that person and take turns verbally expressing all the good things this person has done. They celebrate the individual's good deeds and welcome them back into the tribe. Creating a culture beyond transactional relationships, beyond biases and differences, is essential in creating a culture of belonging and care. A system of care and belonging supports individuals as their authentic selves, their positive contributions to the group, and their relationship and impact on the collective identity of the organization. This leverage of the individual and the group creates a virtuous cycle toward the greatest hope of the organization.

Creating Stronger Work Groups

Inclusion can be transnational and powerful, yet it can be frail and only as strong as the strongest group. For example, when the dominant group no longer has a need for your voice, talents, perspective, or ideas, you can be expelled and excluded from the larger group. Racism is an example of exclusion. Racism prevents reciprocation. To function effectively as a community of inclusion, principals and teachers should focus on how to foster relationships beyond racial differences through respecting and honoring diversity.

Organizations in general are becoming more and more racially and culturally diverse, which increases the need to examine the quality and impact of those relationships within the organization. For example, race impacts relationships and work environments by making it challenging for Black teachers to navigate daily responsibilities and race relations. A study by Smith and Yoshino (2013) involving more than 1,200 participants across five industries revealed that 60 percent of employees engage in what's known as "covering." Covering refers to individuals minimizing identities that are contrary to the mainstream, often resulting in further marginalization of traditionally underrepresented groups. "Covering occurred with greater frequency within groups that have been historically underrepresented" (Smith & Yoshino, 2013). Such glaring statistics reinforce the need to foster and support inclusive cultures of belonging in the workplace.

Organization Culture, Diversity, and Belonging

Organizational culture is the identity, beliefs, and values that influence behavior in an organization. Edgar Schien (1989) best describes organizational culture as "the way we do business around here." For long-time members of an organization, culture often goes unnoticed. *This Is Water*, by David Foster Wallace, draws a connection to daily living in our environments, like fish unaware of the water in which they swim. Wallace (2012) shared, "The most obvious, important realities are often the ones that are hardest to see and talk about." Organizational culture symbolizes the water in which we swim. The water is unnoticed, and members are often unmindful of the essential realities of why the water is important. Organizational culture is more than a vision/mission statement and a strategic plan. Culture is evidence of beliefs and values in actions and interactions. In a report by McKinsey (2015) on diversity in the workplace, "Companies in the top quartile for racial and ethnic diversity are 35 percent more likely to have financial returns above their respective national industry medians." Humans are diverse in a multitude of ways, including culture, race, age, ethnicity, gender, and sexual orientation. Research suggests a best practice of improving capacity and transforming products might be in hiring more women and culturally diverse group members (Díaz-García et al., 2013). Additionally, the most proactive groups are based on life experiences and deep cultural mental models (Garmston & McKanders, 2022). Again, this reinforces the necessity of organizations intentionally cultivating inclusive spaces of belonging that honor and leverage all forms of diversity.

In the *Four Pivots*, Dr. Shawn Ginwright (2022) explores care and belonging and ways of seeing (getting to know others' authentic selves) to help move relationships from transactional to transformative. As we know from Cognitive Coaching, intentional listening is a skill that can be taught and refined. Listening sets the conditions and increases the capacity for care and belonging. The more we see people more fully, the better we understand them. To help people, we must be able to see they are whole. Ginwright (2022) expresses that seeing others more authentically helps move relationships from transactional to transformative. When we are seen and valued, we feel a sense of belonging. In the current economy, where many organizations are challenged with retention following the height of Covid-19, employees want to feel they are contributing to a greater purpose, feel valued, and, in essence, have a sense of belonging. One way to foster belonging in an organization is by implementing Cognitive Coaching and Culturally Proficient Educational Practices.

Talking to One Another in a Diverse Workplace

Dr. Stacie Stanley, superintendent of a suburban district near Minneapolis, Minnesota, along with her team, developed a five-year strategic plan for addressing the needs of all students in the district. The superintendent's leadership team awareness of their own community and their willingness to learn and implement the tools necessary for change focused on equity, diversity, inclusion, and belonging. The framework and skills assisting with implementation and sustainability were Cognitive Coaching and Culturally Proficient Coaching. Working together was contingent upon leveraging the resources of diverse work groups. Organization leaders, consultants, and experts have learned that while making the workplace a calm, safe, diverse, flexible, equitable, inclusive place is necessary, it is certainly not easy. The strategic plan called for clear outcomes focused on full implementation of culturally proficient educational practice throughout the organization. Educational leaders understood the work from a personal and professional level and used benchmarking assessments to monitor for success. The goals were reestablished, and resources reassigned based on those assessments. Culturally proficient leaders from the superintendent's cabinet took responsibility to work together to institutionalize practices of success.

The workplace is complex not because of thingness but because of relationships. Minda Harts, founder and CEO of the Memo, LLC, teaches a talent development course at New York University. She focuses on team success by building psychologically safe environments. One of the management skills Harts emphasizes is being a skillful communicator: knowing when to listen, when to educate, when to offer feedback, and when to model these behaviors. She believes the purpose of managers building excellent communication skills is providing an effective work ethic to impact retention rates and productivity within organizations. Constructive feedback is a skill Harts describes as productive conversation between manager and staff member. Harts shares with her students, "A tip that always works for me is asking myself this question: Will this feedback move our conversation and our organization forward and lead to a resolution, or will my feedback create strife and confusion?" (p. 2). Feedback impacts relationships, and relationships impact productivity (UKG, 2022).

How do we talk to people about changing their language to be more inclusive, especially in the workplace? Some people become defensive when conversations turn to gender identity or sexual orientation. Friendships have been lost, families have been separated, and education has been disrupted because we don't know how to talk to each other or about each other in ways to honor and value people as more inclusive. How did we get to this place of ignoring students in our classrooms, bullying staff members in our workplaces, and creating a hostile work environment against those who claim to be different?

What would our environments be like if we knew how to be more sincere and inclusive irrespective of others' sexual orientation? Katrina Kibben, founder and CEO of Three Ears Media, reminds us that when we know, we behave better. She suggests we start changing the way we behave by rewriting how we learned about some people in our early years. How did we learn about those who didn't fit in? How did we learn the names we called our classmates? Jokes? Books? Movies? Some attempts have been made at rewriting these narratives through policies like "Don't ask, don't tell" and anti-discrimination laws. Yet, the journey is still long and difficult.

Kibben suggests conversations might be different if we started with "Hi. My name is ___. My pronouns are ___. How should I refer to you?" Could it be that simple? When we get people talking, listening, discussing, and telling their stories, by the end of the day, we are building opportunities for inclusion and belonging.

In this current age of divisiveness, fear, anger, and conflict, Margaret Wheatley acknowledges that we have lost productive ways of communicating with each other. As we watch our world leaders, we see them blame each other for problems and conflict. We no longer share resources nor ideas. Wheatley states, "We have lost the capacity to work together to resolve the complex problems that are creating more and more suffering." However, she introduces a way of being that might help bring resolution to our current loss of belonging.

Wheatley describes a five-stage process that originated in ancient Tibet as the Four Karmas (actions).

- The process demands *deep inquiry*: we rely on differences of experience and perception in order to discern actions that might bring sanity to addressing the issue.
- It also requires *humility*: we honor the fact that no one person or group has the answer.
- The process requires *appreciation*: the experiences of all stakeholders are essential to understanding the complexity of the issue.
- It requires *patience*: we take the time to understand diverse perspectives.
- It develops *insight:* we open to collective intelligence that arises as we work well together.

This process is based on *assumptions* that underpin any healthy group process:

- Certainty is the source of positional conflicts.
- Curiosity creates possibilities and new relationships.
- All perspectives are essential but not sufficient—no one person or group understands the problem sufficiently.
- Every perspective, prejudice, and opinion offers information.
- Everybody is an expert about their own experience.
- Respectful listening creates space for both relationships and insights.
- People support what they create; engagement is a necessity.
- Diversity is a life-saving blessing, not a problem.

Five Stages to Solving Complex Problems

Wheatley describes the five Tibetan stages to solving complex problems: "The problem sits in the middle. We are engaged together in developing a rich understanding of its complexity and, from that shared understanding, discerning wise actions. There are five separate activities to complete in sequence. The sequence is important, although one stage may require a lot of time and other stages are moved through more quickly."

- **Stage I.** Cooling, Quieting: symbolized by the circle, time to listen to each other and learn different perspectives, sit in quietness, and experience patience and curiosity.
- **Stage II.** Enriching through Fruitful Opposition: symbolized by the square, take only one side, go deeply with that position, listen respectfully, listening invites confusion, boundaries are loosened, and conversation is possible.
- **Stage III.** Magnetizing Resources is symbolized by the half circle. More information and different perspectives will complete the circle; the emptiness seeks to be filled with new information, and strong pulls will attract likeness.
- **Stage IV.** Precise Destroying is symbolized by the triangle; destruction is intentional and planned rather than reactive and competitive. The focus is on clarity and compassion, not fear or anger.
- **Stage V.** Intelligent Action is symbolized by small circles, focused on solving the problem with current and new resources, becoming better listeners, becoming more open and curious, developing new thinking skills, and learning to work with people we had misunderstood, ignored, or feared. We've become a more intelligent, diverse, inclusive, and confident team.

Wheatley concludes by describing this five-step process for inclusion and belonging by saying,

"If we are to work together more intelligently, we will need to choose processes that evoke our curiosity, humility, generosity, and wisdom. The ultimate benefit is that we learn that it is good, once again, to work together" (p. 11).

References

Díaz-García, C., González-Moreno, A., & Sáez-Martínez, F. J. (2013). Gender diversity within R&D teams: Its impact on radicalness of innovation. *Innovation, 15*(2), 149–160. https://doi.org/10.5172/impp.2013.15.2.149

Garmston, R. J., & McKanders, K. A. (2022). *Cognitive coaching: Developing self-directed leaders and learners* (4th ed.). Rowman & Littlefield.

Ginwright, S. A. (2022). *The four pivots: Reimagining justice, reimagining ourselves.* North Atlantic Books.

McKinsey & Company. (2015). Diversity matters. https://www.mckinsey.com/business-functions/people-and-organizational-performance/our-insights/why-diversity-mattersNuri-

Schien, E. H. (1989). *Organizational culture and leadership: A dynamic view*. Jossey-Bass.

Smith, K., & Yoshino, K. (2013). *Uncovering talent: A new model of inclusion*. Deloitte University Leadership Center for Inclusion. https://www2.deloitte.com/us/en/pages/about-deloitte/articles/uncovering-talent.html

UKG. (2022). Workplace trends 2022: The state of belonging, equity, and inclusion. https://www.ukg.com/resources/article/hr-workforce-management/state-of-belonging-equity-inclusion-2022

Wallace, D. F., Nathan, D., & Blumenbach, U. (2012). *This is water*. Roof Music.

Wheatley, M., & Crinean, G. (2022). Solving complex problems relying on diversity and inclusion: An ancient process of discernment that leads to sane and unified actions. https://margaretwheatley.com/wp-content/uploads/2022/04/Solving-Complex-Problems-Relying-on-Diversity-and-Inclusion.pdf

Leading with Prosocial and Emotional Intelligence

Wendy Baron

6

Building a Prosocial Culture: Lessons from Schools and Businesses (p. 62)

The "New Normal" in Schools and Business (p. 62)

Empowering Individuals through SEL and Emotional Intelligence (p. 62)

Creating Thriving Learning and Work Environments (p. 63)

Case Study: Leadership in Schools and Companies (p. 65)

Supporting Educator and Employee Efficacy (p. 66)

Prosocial Leadership in Schools and Business (p. 66)

Envisioning a Thriving Learning and Working Environment (p. 66)

No significant learning can occur without a significant relationship.
—Dr. James Comer (1995)

Dr. James Comer, a pioneer in social and emotional learning (SEL), recognized in the 1960s that integrating SEL into classrooms could nurture prosocial development in students, helping to alleviate racial trauma and other adverse childhood experiences (ACEs). His insights laid the groundwork for creating environments where emotional intelligence and prosocial behaviors flourish.

Building a Prosocial Culture: Lessons from Schools and Businesses

Prosocial learning fosters behaviors like empathy, cooperation, and inclusivity, which are vital for a harmonious school environment. A prosocial culture reduces aggression, bullying, and emotional distress, creating a safer space where both students and teachers thrive. Similarly, in the business world, leaders who cultivate a prosocial culture often see enhanced team collaboration, reduced conflicts, and improved employee satisfaction.

Consider Satya Nadella, CEO of Microsoft, who transformed the company's culture by emphasizing empathy and collaboration. Nadella's leadership style, rooted in emotional intelligence, shifted Microsoft from a competitive, individualistic environment to one that values teamwork and open communication. This change not only improved the company's internal dynamics but also fueled innovation and growth (Mehtam, 2024).

The "New Normal" in Schools and Business

The post-pandemic era has brought an increase in emotional volatility, with students facing greater challenges in building healthy relationships. The 2023 Education Week report highlighted stress as a major contributor to the youth mental health crisis. Similarly, in the business world, employees are navigating unprecedented stressors—remote work challenges, economic uncertainties, and personal anxieties—making it essential for leaders to prioritize emotional intelligence alongside traditional business acumen.

Leaders like Jacinda Ardern, former prime minister of New Zealand, exemplify how emotional intelligence can guide a nation through crises. Ardern's compassionate leadership during the Covid-19 pandemic fostered trust and resilience among New Zealanders, demonstrating how empathy and clear communication can stabilize and unite communities in times of uncertainty (Friedman, 2020).

Empowering Individuals through SEL and Emotional Intelligence

According to CASEL (Collaborative for Academic, Social and Emotional Learning), SEL is crucial for developing self-awareness, self-management, social awareness, and relationship skills. In schools, SEL fosters a strong sense of identity, agency, and belonging. In business, these same principles apply. Leaders who prioritize emotional intelligence help employees set personal goals, develop resilience, and enhance responsible decision-making capabilities.

Take the example of Howard Schultz (2011), former CEO of Starbucks, who implemented policies that reflect a deep understanding of his employees' needs. Schultz introduced healthcare benefits for part-time workers, recognizing the importance of supporting employees' well-being to foster loyalty and performance. This approach, grounded in emotional intelligence, strengthened the company's culture and brand loyalty.

Creating Thriving Learning and Work Environments

To build environments where individuals—whether students in schools or employees in businesses—can thrive, it's essential to integrate the principles of prosocial and emotional intelligence into everyday practices. This involves several key strategies:

1. **Fostering a sense of belonging:** In both schools and workplaces, individuals need to feel a strong sense of belonging. This can be achieved by cultivating inclusive cultures where diverse perspectives are valued. In schools, teachers can encourage inclusivity through group activities that promote collaboration and mutual respect. In businesses, leaders can promote diversity and inclusion initiatives, ensuring that all employees feel seen and heard.

    For example, Salesforce, under the leadership of CEO Marc Benioff, has been a trailblazer in promoting equality in the workplace. Benioff's commitment to equality and social responsibility has helped create a culture where employees feel valued and connected to the company's mission, leading to higher engagement and innovation (Bridges, 2019).

2. **Encouraging open communication:** Open communication is crucial for building trust and understanding. In schools, this means creating safe spaces where students can express their emotions and thoughts without fear of judgment. Educators can model active listening and empathetic responses to foster a supportive classroom environment. In business, leaders establish clear channels of communication, where employees can share ideas and concerns openly. Regular feedback loops and transparent decision-making processes help build trust and alignment within teams.

Ray Dalio (2017), the founder of Bridgewater Associates, emphasizes radical transparency and open communication in his leadership approach. By encouraging employees to openly discuss mistakes and learn from them, Dalio has created a culture of continuous improvement and trust.

3. **Prioritizing well-being and self-care:** A thriving environment prioritizes the well-being of its members. In schools, this involves integrating SEL into the curriculum and teaching students the importance of self-care and emotional regulation for managing stress and building resilience.

    In the workplace, companies should offer wellness programs that address mental, emotional, and physical health. This might include access to mental health resources, flexible work schedules, and opportunities for physical activity. Google, for example, has long been known for its employee wellness programs, which include on-site fitness centers, healthy food options, and mental health support services. These initiatives not only improve employee well-being but also enhance productivity and job satisfaction (Honest Chops, 2017).

4. **Building emotional intelligence through professional development:** For educators, professional development in SEL can enhance their own ability to effectively manage the many pressures of teaching and prepare them to support students' emotional and social growth. Surveying staff members about their own mental health and students' emotional needs enables school leaders to provide just the right support to teachers.

    Business leaders can benefit from executive coaching and workshops focused on emotional intelligence, helping them to lead with empathy and make more informed, people-centered decisions.

    At Goldman Sachs, the company has implemented emotional intelligence training for its managers, recognizing that these skills are critical for leadership in a fast-paced, high-pressure environment. By equipping leaders with the tools to manage their own emotions and understand the emotions of others, Goldman Sachs fosters a more cohesive and resilient workforce (Psico-smart Editorial Team, 2024).

5. **Promoting collaboration and teamwork:** Collaboration is a cornerstone of both effective learning and successful business operations. In schools, group projects and cooperative learning activities encourage students to work together, share ideas, and support one another's learning. Academic conversations build effective communication skills that are critically important in all relationships.

These experiences teach students the value of teamwork, prepare them for collaborative work environments, and support a lifetime of satisfying relationships with family and friends.

In business, fostering a collaborative culture can lead to greater innovation and problem-solving. Companies like Pixar and IDEO have built their success on a foundation of collaboration, where diverse teams work together to generate creative solutions. Leaders in these companies encourage cross-functional collaboration, ensuring that every team member's voice is heard and valued (Nesirat, 2023; Scarbrough, 2023).

6. **Implementing prosocial leadership:** Prosocial leadership involves leading by example, demonstrating empathy, fairness, and a commitment to the well-being of others. In schools, principals and teachers who model and teach prosocial behaviors create a ripple effect, influencing students to adopt similar behaviors. Bullying and microaggressions that disrupt learning decrease, and attendance and attention in class increase. In business, leaders who prioritize the welfare of their employees and communities foster a culture of trust and loyalty.

Paul Polman, the former CEO of Unilever, is a prime example of a prosocial leader. Polman shifted Unilever's focus toward sustainability and social responsibility, proving that businesses can thrive while making a positive impact on society. His leadership not only enhanced Unilever's brand reputation but also attracted talent who were motivated by the company's values (Dih Kahn, 2023).

Case Study: Leadership in Schools and Companies

At a Santa Cruz elementary school, the fourth and fifth-grade Student Leadership team analyzed data from a recent survey on safety, connection, and emotional experiences. They identified a need for better coping strategies and proposed introducing Peace Kits in classrooms to help students manage difficult situations. Their proactive approach, supported by school staff, underscores the importance of student voice in creating a positive school culture.

In the business realm, Indra Nooyi, former CEO of PepsiCo, used similar strategies to empower employees. She introduced the "Performance with Purpose" initiative, aligning business goals with social responsibility. By involving employees in the decision-making process and encouraging them to contribute ideas, Nooyi fostered a sense of ownership and purpose, driving both employee engagement and business success (Adelaide, 2016).

Supporting Educator and Employee Efficacy

Educator well-being is foundational to a healthy school environment. However, current mental health initiatives often place the burden of self-care on individuals rather than addressing systemic issues. A comprehensive approach to educator efficacy must include emotional awareness, emotional regulation, reflective practice, and strategies for stress management. In business, leaders like Tony Hsieh, the late CEO of Zappos, recognized the importance of creating a supportive work environment. Hsieh prioritized employee happiness, implementing programs that fostered a sense of community and belonging, which in turn boosted productivity and company performance (Mayer, 2020).

Prosocial Leadership in Schools and Business

Effective school leadership plays a crucial role in cultivating a prosocial culture. Leaders with strong social and emotional competence (SEC) create environments where staff, students, and the broader community feel valued and respected. In business, prosocial leadership is equally important.

Jimmy Carter exemplified prosocial leadership through his commitment to humanitarian causes and his empathetic approach to problem-solving. As president of the United States, Carter prioritized human rights, striving to mediate peace and foster global collaboration, as seen in the historic Camp David Accords. Post-presidency, his work with Habitat for Humanity showcased his dedication to improving the lives of underserved communities. Carter's actions reflect a profound understanding of the importance of empathy, compassion, and social responsibility, serving as an inspiring model for leaders in fostering trust and driving positive change (History.com Editors, 2025).

Envisioning a Thriving Learning and Working Environment

To create spaces where everyone flourishes, whether in schools or businesses, we must prioritize collaboration, empathy, and inclusive practices. This vision requires a systemic shift in how we approach education and leadership, integrating a focus on cultivating social and emotional intelligence into the core of our institutions. When students, educators, and employees alike feel connected and supported, they are more engaged, motivated, and successful in their endeavors.

In a classroom setting, a teacher might recognize when a student is feeling overwhelmed and anxious. Support might be in the form of listening and acknowledging feelings; allowing the student to take some time in the "calm corner"; or perhaps referring the student to the school counselor for 1:1 support.

Or, during group work, the teacher notices a student's body language and checks in privately, asking how they're feeling. The student admits they are struggling with the material. The teacher responds empathetically and connects them with a peer for extra help, fostering prosocial behavior by encouraging peer collaboration and reducing the student's stress.

Or, a teacher notices a student verbally teasing another student. The teacher takes a moment to pause and think about what to say. Rather than punishing the student who made the comment, the teacher instead focuses on what was said or done in order to foster growth. The teacher then offers feedback and education to the student(s) by sharing how that comment may have made someone feel, including the teacher, as well as inviting the student(s) to think together about the comment, intentions, and impact on others.

These scenarios illustrate how understanding students' emotions and creating a supportive environment enhances learning, builds positive and supportive relationships, and results in a prosocial culture of thriving.

In a corporate team, a manager exhibiting prosocial leadership might notice rising tension between team members during a project. The manager then arranges a team-building session to encourage open communication and trust-building. During the session, team members are encouraged to share their perspectives in a safe space. As a result, the team repairs relationships, resolves their issues, collaborates more effectively, and becomes more engaged in the project.

This shows how leaders can create a thriving work environment by fostering positive social interactions, which lead to better team dynamics and productivity.

In both educational and business environments, prosocial leadership is not just a pathway to individual and organizational success—it is a catalyst for advancing peace and prosperity on a broader scale. By cultivating empathy, fostering collaboration, and prioritizing the well-being of others, leaders can create inclusive spaces where trust and mutual respect thrive. These qualities are essential for resolving conflicts, promoting equity, and driving innovation. As we navigate the complexities of modern society, the adoption of prosocial leadership principles will be instrumental in building resilient communities and ensuring a brighter, more equitable future for all.

References

Adelaide (2016). *Indra Nooyi's "Performance with Purpose" strategy: A lesson in leadership*. Forbes. https://www.forbes.com/sites/forbesleadershipforum/2016/10/04/indra-nooyes-performance-with-purpose-lessons-in-leadership/

Bridges, F. (2019, November 26). *Salesforce Co-CEO Marc Benioff dispenses advice on building a purposeful and profitable business in new book 'Trailblazer'*. Forbes. https://www.forbes.com/sites/francesbridges/2019/11/26/salesforce-co-ceo-marc-benioff-dispenses-advice-on-building-a-purposeful-and-profitable-business-in-new-book-trailblazer/?ctpv=searchpage

Comer, J, (1995). Lecture given at Education Service Center, Region IV. Houston, TX.

Dalio, R. (2017). *Principles: Life and work*. Simon & Schuster. So Brief. https://sobrief.com/books/principles

Dih Kahn, A. (2023, April 18). *What can we learn from a leader who change the way we do business?* LinkedIn. https://www.linkedin.com/pulse/what-can-we-learn-from-leader-who-change-way-do-andr%C3%A9a-dih-kahn/

Friedman, U. (2020, April 19). *New Zealand's prime minister may be the most effective leader on the planet*. The Atlantic. https://www.theatlantic.com/politics/archive/2020/04/jacinda-ardern-new-zealand-leadership-coronavirus/610237/

History.com Editors. (2025). "Jimmy Carter." *A&E Television Networks*.

Honest Chops. (2017). *Google's corporate wellness programs*. IBS Center for Management Research. https://www.icmrindia.org/Short Case Studies/Human Resource Management/CLHR045.htm - :~:text=In%202015%2C%20Greatist%20considered%20US,a%20prerequisite.%E2%80%9D

Mayer, K. (2020, December 3). *How Tony Hsieh inspired a focus on workplace culture*. HR Executive. https://hrexecutive.com/how-tony-hsieh-inspired-a-focus-on-workplace-culture/ - :~:text=%E2%80%9CHsieh%20famously%20set%20cultivating%20a,designed%20to%20keep%20employees%20happy.

Mehtam, S. (2024, June 3). *Satya Nadella's 3-word description of Microsoft's culture should inspire leaders to be learners*. Fast Company. https://www.fastcompany.com/91133383/microsoft-ceo-satya-nadella-3-word-description-microsoft-culture-leadership

Nesirat, Y. (2023). *To infinity and beyond: The incredible success story of Pixar through teamwork and collaboration*. Medium. https://medium.com/leadership-by-design/to-infinity-and-beyond-the-incredible-success-story-of-pixar-animation-studios-through-teamwork-c86eed815b6

Psico-smart Editorial Team (2024, August 28). *Integrating emotional intelligence into managerial skills development programs*. Blogs.psico Smart. https://blogs.psico-smart.com/blog-integrating-emotional-intelligence-into-managerial-skills-development-programs-166307 - :~:text=Another%20compelling%20case%20comes%20from,did%20not%20receive%20the%20training.

Scarbrough, R. (2023). *IDEO: Revolutionizing design—a look into their impact and innovations*. Design Does That. https://designdoesthat.com/ideo-revolutionizing-design-a-look-into-their-impact-and-innovations/ - :~:text=IDEO%20firmly%20believes%20in%20the,fresh%20insights%20and%20innovative%20ideas.

Schultz, H. (2011). *Onward: How Starbucks fought for its life without losing its soul*. Rodale Books.

Section III

Applications of Cognitive Coaching's Principles and Values in Other Disciplines

Introduction

Cognitive Coaching initially emerged in the 1980s for coaching teachers and other school personnel. In this section, readers will discover ways CC principles and skills are being put into practice by leaders trained in Cognitive Coaching in fields as diverse as health care, music, and even religion.

But what is Cognitive Coaching contributing to other fields? Certainly not the coaching protocols used in schools, the appreciation of what goes on the minds of teachers when they teach nor methods of assessing coaching performance. Being used in other fields instead are the values, aims, principles, states of mind, and skills we define as the learned ability to act with determined results with good execution often within a given amount of time, energy, or both. These are the characteristics that lend Cognitive Coaching its fruitfulness and can be productively used in other disciplines.

Enhancing Mind-Body Awareness

EJ Zebro and Bena Kallick

7

Tuning Up Your Sensors: Learning How to Read the Signals (p. 72)

Habits of Movement and Habits of Mind (p. 73)

The Habits of Movement You Build through Deliberate Practice (p. 74)

What Real Strength Looks Like (p. 76)

A Culture of Connection: Inside and Out (p. 78)

Every gym member has their own reason for hitting the gym and working out. A forty-something-year-old golfer comes to improve his backswing. A senior comes to improve his health and lengthen his lifespan. A mother of young children seeks ways to improve her resilience and reduce her stress after the pandemic. A college tennis player, who dreams of one day becoming a pro athlete, comes in to work out an issue with her shoulder that limits her ability to serve.

How does TAP Strength, a holistic gym, coach all these people with varied backgrounds in developing body-mind awareness? How can they learn to identify old and counterproductive habits and replace them with new, healthier ones that will help them successfully stay in the game of life?

We often hear the terms "psychological safety" and "physical safety" used separately; however, these ideas are more intertwined than previously thought. It is this combination of mind and body awareness that sets TAP Strength apart.

EJ Zebro and Bena Kallick have been working together for the past twenty years. EJ is the founder of TAP Strength, a chiropractor, a personal trainer, and the creator of the *Habits of Movement*. Bena is an educator and coauthor of many books on *Habits of Mind* (Costa & Kallick, 2008). Through this partnership, EJ and Bena have explored how the combination of mind and body can help us to age and develop gracefully as we build a combination of mind and movement. As a result, it is becoming clear that central to the connection between psychological and physical safety is about building competence, confidence, and self-efficacy.

This can be achieved by:

- sharing a descriptive language that is associated with each of the habits we to grow our cognition
- collaborating in an inclusive community that provides a sense of belonging
- trusting the expert guidance from teachers who know how to educate and challenge body and mind awareness and connections

Tuning Up Your Sensors: Learning How to Read the Signals

The first, and most important, step in body awareness is to learn how to read your body. Mind-body awareness requires employing the habit of gathering data through the senses. We used to think of our senses as our ability to see, touch, taste, smell, and hear. However, through recent research in neuroscience, we have expanded our knowledge about the senses:

- The five senses (see, touch, taste, smell, and hear) are now referred to as *exteroception*—what you notice in your external environment.
- An additional sense that is essential to understanding our body's position in time and space has been uncovered—*proprioception*.
- There are two other ways we sense that contribute to our overall body awareness. Our ability to understand our world from the internal cues of our body such as thirst, hunger, fear, heart rate, respiration, and many more gives us an internal perception of our external world and is referred to as *interoception*.
- And finally, our perception of what causes us stress and distress often directly affecting the way we move and interact and even breathe in

the external world, which is called *nociception*. This is our general perception of pain and how we process that pain in both a physical and emotional state.

It is a healthy balance of interoception, exteroception, proprioception, and nociception that encompasses your overall mind-body awareness.

Fascia is the connective tissue that envelops our internal organs, muscles, nerves, veins, and bones, giving structure to our body and making all connections possible. Further developments in research have demonstrated that the fascial network is the main organ in the human body responsible for transmitting and organizing sensory information from internal and external cues. This fascial network is ultimately how we interpret the world around us.

These scientific contributions broadened the possibilities for becoming more physically and mentally aware. It changed the way professional athletes train for high-quality performance. And, as is demonstrated at TAP Strength, it has shown that increasing mind-body awareness can help anyone improve their general functional performances. Whether it be in sports, sitting at a computer, or standing in a classroom all day, mind-body awareness has an impact in helping us become more efficacious in whatever we choose.

EJ calls this space "TAP," which stands for *Train Awareness Performance*. Unlike comparable gyms, TAP is founded on redefining strength and building confidence in body and mind through an expanded understanding of the senses and its cognitive counterpart of metacognition (thinking about your thinking), Habits of Movement, and Habits of Mind. When you work out at TAP Strength, you intentionally practice how to TAP in through body and mind awareness of the senses and specific movements that create neural pathways that grow as you improve your proficiency with the movements. The benefit of these intentional workouts continues after you leave the holistic gym and TAP out. Through deliberate practice of mobility and stability through specific movements, we start to build the habits. The stronger the habits, the stronger the neural pathways of mind and body. We are attuning ourselves to effortless action—referred to as being "in the flow."

Habits of Movement and Habits of Mind

Strength is both mental and physical and with consistent training, we learned how to powerfully link the Habits of Mind to the Habits of Movement. For John Dewey, "habit" isn't simply an action that repeats itself. It is, instead, an "active disposition." Habits are shaped by social interactions and our responses to our environments. And once a habit is established through neural pathways, we no longer deliberate about our actions; we simply react. As a result of our social norms, we have reinforced some habits through common misunderstandings. For example, some people believe in a common cliche, "no pain, no gain," as if that is a key indicator of building strength. Suppose, instead, we became mindful and asked ourselves, what would be the best possible outcome for me in a workout? When I first met EJ, he suggested that if I worked with him, he would help me grow to be as functional in strength as I personally might be capable of. I loved that goal! It sounded like a protection from pain rather than a gain. It is about recognizing that some repetitions might be causing pain and becoming mindful about why that pain exists to get to the root cause and change any habits that are counterproductive.

The Habits of Movement You Build through Deliberate Practice

From the Trainer's Perspective

1. *Persisting:* activating the strength inside us; it only becomes a habit with consistency of practice.
2. *Balance:* creating connections in the body. Center yourself—take the time to center your body and your mind—it is as easy as shifting from one position to another.
3. *Stability:* building a strong foundation for your core. Take the time to find your core and focus your breathing to keep the focus on your core.
4. *Power:* controlling force and generating energy efficiently. Use your body to store energy and release energy, building your power with each movement.
5. *Flow:* coordinating whole body movements effortlessly. Find the rhythm of your body so that you can move with grace both inside and outside of the gym.
6. *Elasticity:* growing stronger connective tissues and improved range of motion. As your elasticity improves, so does your ability to bounce back not only from injuries but from near injuries as well.
7. *Recovering:* bouncing back from stress and tension before it builds. Set aside ample time for self-care strategies that restore both the body and the mind.
8. *Growing:* believing that we have the ability to harness this growth of our body and our mind.

When we set the intention for increased physical and mental growth, we can achieve great things through improved neural pathways and connections.

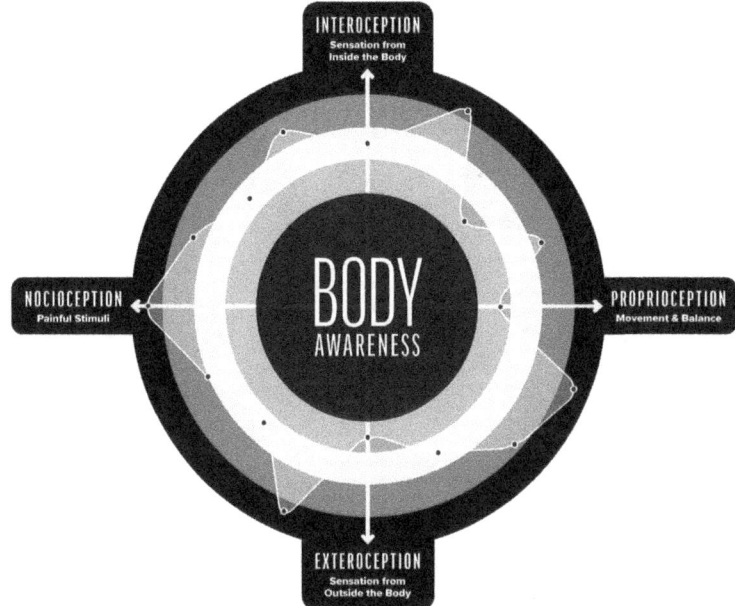

Figure 7.1 What is body awareness? Dr. EJ Zebro.

From a Client's Perspective, Using Habits of Mind

1. *Persisting:* changes in your body functions are inevitable. You need to stay the course with your exercise.
2. *Thinking flexibly:* you must make adaptations in terms of your expectations of what you can do.
3. *Listening with understanding and empathy:* you need to have a trainer who can be attentive to who you are and what you are trying to accomplish.
4. *Striving for accuracy*: the word "striving" is important here. You won't always do the exercises with precision, but you have a good idea about what you are striving for, as the pictures of the exercises in this book suggest.
5. *Gathering data through all senses:* pay attention to all the possible cues that can help you know more about how you move.
6. *Taking responsible risks:* this is critical to the partnership with the trainers. The client often hesitates to try a move that they don't think they can do. Through practice in the protective space of the holistic gym, they learn to trust the encouragement to meet new challenges.
7. *Remaining open to continuous learning:* there is always something new to discover and new challenges to manage. The clients amaze themselves at what they're capable of doing!

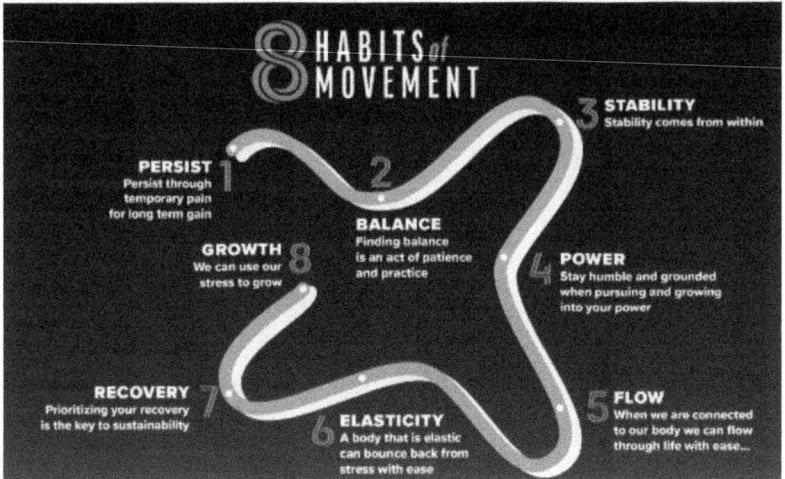

Figure 7.2 Eight Habits of Movement. Dr. EJ Zebro.

What Real Strength Looks Like

As EJ works with a client, he assesses her for strengths and imbalances. He considers her goal to feel as strong, capable, and independent as they work in a school with difficult staircases. He sets up a challenge to build her confidence through a series of lunges that require her proprioception. She must step up on a ledge, do a lunge, and then balance on one leg. She then steps down and repeats the cycle once again. With guidance, she is learning how to build strength in her legs, control her core, and stay connected to her breath. After some trial and error and reassessing, she becomes able to perform these moves and starts to build confidence in her capacity to endure through repetitive, stressful conditions.

When she goes to school the next day, she climbs the stairs without thinking about the details of what her body is doing. She is in the flow—there is a sense of automaticity in which she appreciates that she is in the moment without continuous mental rehearsal telling her what to think and do. She is able to TAP in while working with EJ, thinking about the specifics of each movement and increasing her strength and neural pathways, allowing her to TAP out and move more effortlessly in the world outside of TAP Strength.

Over time, these coaching sessions serve as a cognitive road map when there is a disruption as the body moves through time and space. When that happens, there is a power to stop, take a moment to be centered, remember what you have learned in the training session, and assess, adjust, and recover.

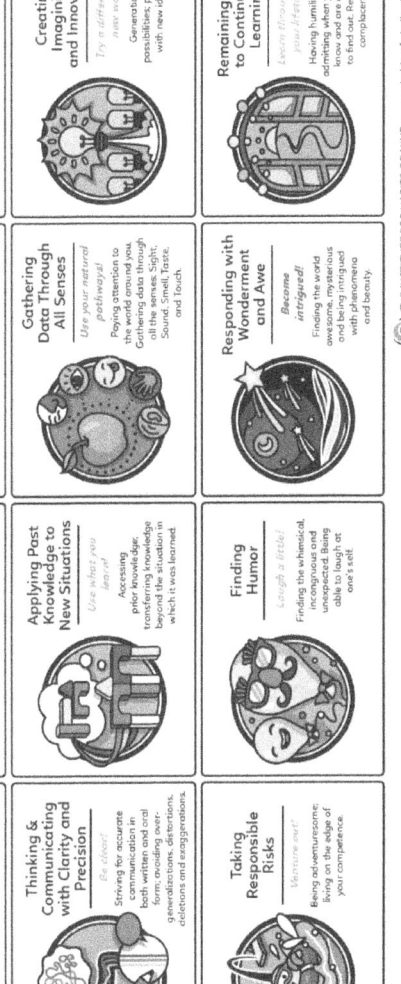

Figure 7.3 Habits of Mind. Institute for Habits of Mind.

A Culture of Connection: Inside and Out

When people join TAP Strength, they feel immediately included and in a place that is psychologically and physically safe in which they can grow. Everyone on the TAP team embodies a set of core values. They embody a purpose of guiding people along their journey of physical and mental well-being. What guides the team is the following set of core values that each embodies as they work with one another as well as with their clients:

- Being present
- Staying connected with mutual trust and respect
- Developing open and honest communication
- Having fun and maintaining a sense of humor
- Thinking creatively and innovatively
- Fostering a growth mindset
- Listening with compassion and empathy

As a result of these coaching behaviors, TAP becomes an efficacious community in which each client feels a sense of belonging. People are encouraged to take the risks of new learning in a noncompetitive environment. Everyone is recognized for their unique talents and strengths as well as challenged to grow new competencies and skills. Clients observe the team modeling the behaviors while teaching and are responsive to the advice and support from a team that has experience with curiosity for continuous learning. The hope is that when people go to their workplaces, they might build their own core values, embody the mind-body practices that they are growing, and become role models for others. Being a part of the TAP Strength culture fosters connections to the work inside the gym and outside into the lives of a diverse population of thinkers and movers.

Reference

Costa, A., & Kallick, B. (2008). *Learning and leading with habits of mind: 16 essential characteristics for success.* ASCD.

Cognitive Coaching in Spiritual Accompaniment
Father Luis J. González

8

Cognitive Coaching in Christian Spiritual Accompaniment (p. 80)

Cognitive Coaching for Spiritual Accompaniment (p. 81)

Cognitive Coaching in Mexico (p. 81)

Cognitive Coaching at the Pontifical Faculty of the Teresianum in Rome, Italy (p. 82)

Cognitive Coaching at the University of Mysticism in Ávila, Spain (p. 82)

Formators for the Mystical Experience (p. 84)

Conclusion (p. 85)

I was born in Guadalajara, Mexico, in 1942. I have been a Carmelite since 1961 and a priest since 1969. Since then, I have completed PhDs in spiritual theology, counseling, and psychology. I have worked as a counselor and a psychologist in Mexico, Nairobi, and Rome. I have also worked as a professor at the Teresianum, which is the Carmelite university in Rome. In my classes in Mexico, I had the opportunity to study with Carl Rogers, whose work greatly influenced the development of Cognitive Coaching (CC).

My first contact with Cognitive Coaching took place in the green warmth of a corner of Africa in 1997. Near the place where I had my first planning conversation, a brook was flowing, which cheered us with its singing among the rocks. The tropical vegetation with its coconut palms and lush flowers created a festive and joyful natural setting.

My cognitive coach was Dr. Jenny Edwards, whose PhD research was directly related to CC. She had come from Denver, Colorado, to Morogoro, Tanzania, because a friend of mine, José Rodríguez Assemat, had recommended that she come. In those years, I was organizing summer courses for that area as part of the Discalced Carmelite community that had one of its missions in Tanzania. The participants were mostly teachers and Christian missionaries.

Near the end, during the afternoon break, I mentioned some of the teachings of the mystic St. John of the Cross. I expressed my desire to live his teachings even better. Jenny then offered to coach me on how to do that.

We had a short coaching session that lasted approximately twenty minutes. She used the tools of CC with which I was not acquainted. I communicated, with authenticity and confidence, some elements of my personal spiritual life.

My surprise was enormous at the end of the planning conversation. I could not believe I had had a real spiritual accompaniment session like the ones I used to have with Fr. Camillo Maccise, superior general of the Carmelites of the world at that time. I did not understand how a coaching conversation, which I considered as a tool to improve professional performance at work, could have turned into a spiritual colloquium.

Without knowing that Jenny had a PhD and not knowing that her doctoral dissertation had been on CC, I invited her to give a course on pedagogy in the teaching of spirituality at the Pontifical Faculty of the Teresianum in Rome in the autumn of 1997. She continued coaching me while she was there.

Two years later, I had the opportunity to start my training as a cognitive coach with her. I already knew from experience that the tools of this method of coaching—silence, paraphrasing, questions—together with conversation maps and other complementary techniques lent themselves extremely well to spiritual accompaniment. I had learned this from experience and not as a result of a theoretical lesson on accompaniment.

Cognitive Coaching in Christian Spiritual Accompaniment

To make sense of my previous experience and how I came to CC through Christianity, it is important to briefly place myself in the context of the Christian faith. So here are a few of my beliefs:

Jesus of Nazareth is the focus of my faith. I believe that God is a community of love in three persons: Father, Son, and Spirit. I also believe that the Holy Spirit was poured out by God on Jesus when He was baptized by John the Baptist (Mt. 3:16-17; Mk 1:10-11). After that, the Spirit guided Jesus throughout His life even to the cross where He offered Himself, moved by the Holy Spirit (Heb. 9:14). Jesus triumphed over evil, pain, and death with His resurrection. God raised him up through the power of His Spirit.

With these core beliefs, it is understandable that we Christians are convinced that the Holy Spirit, God, and Jesus guide human beings. To me, the Holy Spirit is an inner Guide who convinces and impels people to do good through His tenderness, wisdom, and love.

Cognitive Coaching for Spiritual Accompaniment

What makes CC perfect for spiritual accompaniment in the Christian faith is that CC leaves the person free to let himself or herself be guided by the Spirit of Jesus because the cognitive coach avoids three behaviors:

1. giving advice or recommendations,
2. sharing one's own experience or emotions, and
3. meddling in the person's life out of curiosity or desire to help.

By contrast, the cognitive coach focuses entirely on the person. With the tools of CC—silence, paraphrasing, asking mediating questions—the coach acts as a mediator between the person and his thinking, the person and his resources, and the person and others (Costa & Garmston, 2016). If the person requires it—as was my case in Morogoro, Tanzania—the coach mediates between the person and his or her faith, the person and the Spirit, and the person and the motions of the same Spirit to enable the person to take action.

The latter is, properly speaking, what is understood in many sectors of the ecclesiastical world as spiritual accompaniment. This explains the inclusion of CC in the theological-spiritual formation that Jenny and I have been offering in Mexico, Rome, and Spain.

Cognitive Coaching in Mexico

Jenny and I first offered Cognitive Coaching in Mexico in 2000 in Guadalajara, Mexico. Always in the context of the promotion of spirituality carried out by the Discalced Carmelites of Mexico and copresenting with Dr. Jenny, we have offered—in Spanish—the basic seminar of CC in different cities of

Mexico. The aim of the CC trainings was to provide spiritual accompanists with an effective instrument for building deep relationships with people.

Cognitive Coaching at the Pontifical Faculty of the Teresianum in Rome, Italy

In the 2000–1 academic year at the Teresianum in Rome, as a result of the International Congress of Spiritual Theology inspired by Fr. Rafael Checa, I began to offer optional courses on the Pastoral Care of Spirituality. I was convinced that CC would be a powerful tool for people who were doing spiritual accompaniment for individuals and groups. As a result, in the autumn of 2000, Jenny Edwards offered the first CC seminar at the Pontifical Faculty of the Teresianum. It was a great opportunity for me that she gave me the chance to copresent at the training because of my slightly better Italian. This accelerated my assimilation of CC.

In 2003, I published my first book on CC in Spanish called *Cognitive Coaching: Greater Rational, Emotional and Spiritual Intelligence* (González, 2003) showing it as a wonderful tool for cultivating rational, emotional, and spiritual intelligence. The following year, I published another book to show how CC could foster optimism in people (González, 2004).

Also in 2003, at the Theological Faculty of the Teresianum, I started a three-year program, twelve hours per week, of Spiritual Counseling. The school was affiliated with the Italian Society of Counseling, which was associated with the European Society of Counseling.

Without any hesitation, I believed that CC was fundamental to the course. The training of spiritual counselors requires a style of relationship focusing on the person, a style of treatment that leaves room for the person's relationship with the transcendent Being or with the God of their own faith.

The three-year Spiritual Counseling program included the basic CC seminar with Jenny present and a CC practice every fortnight for three hours. It also included supervised CC practice every two weeks for three hours. As a result, the students were immersed in CC every week, either as a simple practice or as supervision. Unfortunately, in 2020, the Teresianum decided to close the specialization due to the Covid-19 pandemic.

Cognitive Coaching at the University of Mysticism in Ávila, Spain

Another area of application of CC to spiritual accompaniment is taking place in Ávila, Spain. The Centro Internacional Teresiano-Sanjuanista (CITeS), better known as the University of Mysticism, has been offering a short program for people who do spiritual accompaniment since 2008. In light of the experience at the Teresianum in Rome, the organizers included the CC as part of this training.

From the year 2023, at the request of the alumni of the spiritual accompaniment courses (AcEs), the University of Mysticism now offers the Advanced Seminar in CC. Dr. Jenny Edwards offers training, and I copresent with her.

We offer CC in Ávila because of the experiences of St. Teresa of Ávila, foundress of the Carmelites, together with the mystic John of the Cross. She had a triple experience of spiritual accompaniment at the time of her definitive spiritual conversion as a Carmelite nun in the Monastery of the Incarnation in Ávila, Spain, between 1554 and 1555.

The first spiritual director of St. Teresa of Ávila used an authoritarian style of giving her spiritual accompaniment. He gave her directive advice. Gaspar Daza told St. Teresa what she should do. The result was catastrophic. She wrote, "For the affliction I felt in seeing that I did not do—nor did it seem I could do—that which he told me would have been enough to make me lose hope and give up everything" (St. Teresa of Ávila, 1987, p. 204).

Her reaction shows a total drop in her level of efficacy in her spirit. She had a total loss of hope, the inclination to give up, and the decision, almost, to abandon the path of spiritual development as a Carmelite nun.

Fortunately for her, the second companion, a married layman named Don Francisco de Salcedo, provided spiritual accompaniment to Teresa using a democratic style (St. Teresa of Ávila, 1987). He shared his own spiritual experience and gave suggestions and support to the young Carmelite. She was comforted and encouraged to move forward; however, he did not quite understand her and recommended that she talk with a Jesuit priest.

The 23-year-old Fr. Diego de Cetina, who was faithful to the teachings of St. Ignatius of Loyola in the spiritual exercises, used an empathic style that was centered on the person and his Christian faith (St. Teresa of Ávila, 1987). He immediately discerned that the Carmelite nun was moved by a good spirit. Her mystical experiences proved to be authentic.

The noun or adjective *mystical* means experience of the "mystery." The term "mystery" has been chosen by phenomenologists of religion to refer to the absolute Being, the supreme Good, the Creator or the God of the great spiritual traditions. For Teresa, it was the experience of the God revealed by Jesus of Nazareth.

It is amazing what Fr. Cetina achieved in Teresa by using strategies found in CC. The extraordinary impact on her seems incredible. She wrote: "He guided me by means that seemed to change me completely. What a great thing it is to understand a soul. . . . He left me consoled and encouraged" (St. Teresa of Ávila, 1987, p. 208). Then she showed the surprising elevation of her state of efficacy, thanks to the means he used.

> My soul was left so docile from this confession that it seemed to me there was nothing for which I wouldn't prepare myself. As a consequence I began to make many changes, although the confessor didn't press me; rather it seemed that he thought all the changes of little importance. And this urged me more because he guided my soul by stressing the love of God and allowed freedom and used no pressure if I didn't set about doing things out of love. (St. Teresa of Ávila, 1987, p. 209).

Those who know CC immediately notice the alignment of the Jesuit's style just described with the philosophy and tools of CC.

- He showed understanding through empathy, with perhaps some paraphrases.
- It seems that the Jesuit let Teresa be herself.
- He let her be free: Teresa could be self-directed.
- The confessor did not press her. She could make conscious decisions with skill and flexibility.
- She imposed on herself out of love what she decided and did. She was self-directing.
- She showed extraordinary efficacy. "It seemed to me there was nothing for which I wouldn't prepare myself" (St. Teresa of Ávila, 1987, p. 209).
- She showed efficacy and skill. "I began to make many changes" (St. Teresa of Ávila, 1987, p. 209).

Cognitive Coaching, it seems to me, uses, refines, systematizes, and operationalizes the methods the young Jesuit used with Teresa of Ávila, with spectacular results.

Formators for the Mystical Experience

In May 2024, the University of Mysticism launched a new master's program to train people who want to accompany others in their spiritual formation. The formators for the mystical experience will study for a master's degree, which will enable them to accompany the growth of people in relationships of faith, hope, and love with God according to their own religious faith. Students will also learn biblical, theological, mystical, psychological, sociological, and environmental subjects to accompany the formation of people who want to experience God's love, joy, and peace.

CC and spiritual accompaniment fit together in a—I would say—perfect way. As a result, the program for trainers for the mystical experience includes Cognitive Coaching. It seems to be, together with Carl Rogers' Person-Centered Approach (Rogers, 2021), the best combination of skills to help people be open to the eternal Spirit.

Students will receive the basic CC seminar at the beginning of the academic year. Each month, they will have one day of pure practice and supervision. This monthly practice will be extended in the following two years to expand and incorporate the activities and tools of CC. Before that, at the end of the first academic year, they will attend the Advanced CC training.

Conclusion

When someone who knows the experience of Teresa of Ávila with the 23-year-old Jesuit Diego Cetina asks me, "What is Cognitive Coaching?" I reply that Cognitive Coaching is a training that enables people to have the capacity that made Father Cetina an amazing instrument of the Spirit with regard to Teresa. I add that I imagine that God, through His Spirit that is always active in the human heart, asked Art Costa and Bob Garmston, in the early 1980s, to develop a training—including books—to train priests, religious, and laypeople to accompany others with the human and spiritual effectiveness with which Fr. Cetina accompanied Teresa of Ávila.

With this conviction in my heart, every time I meet Art or Bob, I repeat, with admiration and gratitude, my certainty of faith: "For all eternity, God will reward you for having created CC for the human and spiritual development of thousands of children, young people, and adults."

References

Costa, A. L., & Garmston, R. J. (with Hayes, C., & Ellison, J.). (2016). *Cognitive coaching: Developing self-directed leaders and learners*. Rowman & Littlefield.

González, L. J. (2003). *Coaching cognitivo: Mayor inteligencia racional emotive y spiritual*. Ediciones del Teresianum.

González, L. J. (2004). *Coaching cognitivo: Escuela de optimiso*. Ediciones Duruelo.

Rogers, C. (2021). *Client-centered therapy: Its current practice, implications and theory* (70th anniversary edition). Robinson.

St. Teresa of Ávila. (1987). *The collected works of St. Teresa of Ávila* (Vol. 1) (K. Kavanaugh & O. Rodriguez, Trans.). ICS Publications.

Coaching in Health Care

John Clarke

History (p. 88)

Recommendations (p. 93)

> It takes practice . . . but for most people, the feeling of having been listened to—deeply and without judgment—is validating.
>
> —Dr. Ronald Epstein

Dr. Arthur Costa recently stated that Cognitive Coaching has value for any organization that values "thinking, continuous learning and empathic service." The universality of the intention, nature, and impact of Cognitive Coaching has been evident for many years. Specifically, the intuitive and experiential perspective that this body of work has a place in the world of health professionals was the impetus for some earlier and ongoing work in this sector.

In the beginning, Costa and Garmston developed Cognitive Coaching to improve the process and effectiveness of teaching; in other words, to help teachers "teach better, and to look beyond performance at self-actualization, self-directedness." Their model was not about telling people what to do. Coaches intervened at the point of and in support of the teacher's thinking. They envisioned teachers who were self-reliant and autonomous, and who were reflective practitioners in the service of their students. Over time, the fundamental beliefs, the intention, and the guiding principles of Cognitive

Coaching remained the same. However, as needs changed at both individual and system levels, the design and delivery required adaptivity.

Learners, their teachers, and the environments in which learning takes place have shifted and will continue to be in flux, so the opportunities for learning about the work of Cognitive Coaching itself exist. This potentially powerful place is any context where people engage in learning, have conversations about, and assume responsibility for their own learning.

Health care, like many other sectors, has learning at its core. Declarative and technical knowledge abound. Procedural knowledge and processes are essential as well. Many physicians and health care professionals are required to mentor or build capacity and self-directedness in their colleagues, students, and paraprofessionals. Care that is centered on the patient is of high quality and that has effective outcomes also requires that patients learn about and refine their own health management conditions. The intention and capabilities to do this in a sustainable way lie in Cognitive Coaching.

The heart of education is the growth, development, and self-directed lifelong learning of learners of all ages. Health care, while often thought of as "doing to" people (as in emergency medicine), has a large element that is focused on the growth, development, and self-directed healthy living of all individuals. Both sectors rely on the ongoing emergence of skilled professionals who are in the service of others. They also both rely on the development of reflective, progressive, and impactful practice. Medical professionals, such as physicians, are trained in a vast base of scientific, procedural, technical, and often life-saving knowledge. They are also required to mentor medical students, create and facilitate professional teams, engage in meaningful ways with patients and families, and manage and adjust to the changing health care landscape. A specific example of the complexity and duality of the nature of a physician's role was provided by our colleague, Margie Sills-Maerov. She suggested that "it is a technical undertaking to help a patient learn to monitor, interpret and manage their blood sugar levels. That is a technical conversation. It is a different and an adaptive challenge to help someone learn to live with diabetes. That is a coaching conversation." Similarly, the world of the occupational therapist, for example, is centered on supporting patients in becoming self-managing often in light of life-changing events.

History

The application of Cognitive Coaching to noneducational settings was an important focus for our late friend, mentor, and colleague, John Dyer. He stated, "I have taught coaching and witnessed its successful application in a broad range of fields including heavy oil mining, supervision of hairdressing school, human resources, environmental sciences, natural gas transmission, nursing and manufacturing" (2003). In 2005, John and I presented the Cognitive Coaching Foundation Seminar to a group of health professionals at the University of Alberta, Edmonton, Alberta, Canada. The seminar was part of the training offered, at that time, by the Center for Cognitive Coaching. This cohort was comprised of individuals from the fields of Workmen's Compensation, nursing, pharmaceutical sales, human resources, and paramedical instruction. It also included one school principal. All participants completed the seminar and, for University of Alberta academic compliance, were required to submit a journal based on their learning experience and an anecdotal assessment of their application of this learning and the impact of Cognitive Coaching on their professional practice. The results were anecdotal in nature and overwhelmingly positive. This was the beginning of the formal integration of Cognitive Coaching in health care in Canada.

Consequently, with John Dyer's encouragement, materials were designed to customize language, contextual examples, and research references to support a learning environment familiar to noneducational professionals. These resources are now the property of Thinking Collaborative LLC, the organization created in 2013 to house the Center for Adaptive Schools and the Center for Cognitive Coaching. The work with health care organizations has continued.

In 2015, Cognitive Coaching was reintroduced in Alberta through Alberta Health Services. This was a cooperative effort between Thinking Collaborative and Alberta Health Services. In a paper published in the Canadian Society of Physician Leaders, Sills-Maerov wrote,

> As part of continuing professional development, a number of health service agencies in Alberta pooled resources to fund training for improvement professionals and change leaders in the province and test the effectiveness of Cognitive Coaching. We tested the training with two cohorts of 40 improvement professionals and health care leaders. We were quite hesitant at first, as the training required eight (full) days over the course of eight months or so. However, once we all completed the first two days, we quickly realized why it would take eight days: it consisted of skill building, not teaching. It was about learning, testing, practicing, and internalizing. The way it was structured allowed for thinking to be shifted, and then behaviour followed. (CanMeds, 2015 p.5)

We completed qualitative and quantitative evaluations of the participants, looking at self-efficacy, skill acquisition, and application and practicality in the health care environment. Participants experienced a shift in how they looked at their role: they found that they used the skills in high-stress or conflictual situations with success, and it changed the way team members interacted and worked with each other. They had a greater sense of being effective in helping others with change. Instead of having to have the answers about a change, they were instead drawing the answers out of the teams that they were supporting, and they were having a greater impact. They moved away from being "problem solvers" to acting as coaches who enhanced the thinking of others and grew teams and collaborative partnerships" (M. Sills-Maerov, unpublished action research, 2015–2018).

- A participant in one of these groups, offered through Alberta Health Services, commented that her learning through Cognitive Coaching "had changed the nature of every professional conversation in our office."
- One physician commented that an observable consequence from her learning was the positive change in the culture of her family practice clinic.

In 2019, the University of Alberta, Faculty of Medicine and Dentistry, Office of Lifelong Learning, offered the Foundation Seminar to physicians and health care professionals. This cohort, and the work in Canada, came to a grinding halt in March of 2020 due to the Covid-19 pandemic. It would be two years before in-person professional development reemerged in Canada. The work in Cognitive Coaching has since reengaged. Presently, the Foundation Seminar is being provided to primary care networks in Alberta.

Cognitive Coaching was introduced to the Royal College of Physicians and Surgeons of Canada in February 2020. However, with the cessation of in-person learning in March 2020, the challenge was to respond to the growing interest and identified need for coaching for health care professionals and to access virtual platforms to deliver the work. Cognitive Coaching was and is an in-person model. As stated earlier in being adaptable, a professional program was developed out of the evolving need to address the pandemic as well as the overall challenges to provide continuing professional development in health care across a variety of platforms. The professional learning program that evolved was Coaching in Health Care (Clarke, Irons and Sills-Maerov 2019). This design aligned with the values, principles, and skills of Cognitive Coaching (Costa and Garmston, 2016). It also was driven by the intention of human communication central to nondirective counseling (Rogers) and Interpersonal Confirmation Theory (Siefert). The latter identifies the value of the recognition, acknowledgment, and endorsement of another person. This endorsement was also embedded in the design where the identity of the participant was held constant during the training. A self-exploration was provided at the end of the program to allow participants the opportunity to identify how the skills and mindsets explored impacted their own professional identity as a physician or health care professional. The central theme in all this work, including Coaching in Health Care, is the assumption that the person being supported has the potential and resources they need to be self-managing. The new model also values, supports, invites, explores, and extends thinking.

The Royal College of Physicians and Surgeons relies on the CanMEDS physician competency framework to guide the educational and practice standards of the College. Competency as a communicator requires that "physicians enable patient-centered therapeutic communication by exploring the patient's symptoms, which may be suggestive of disease, and by actively listening to the patient's experience of his or her illness. Physicians explore the patient's perspective, including his or her fears, ideas about the illness, feelings about the impact of the illness, and expectations of health care and health-care professionals." This competency cites active listening, empathy, expert verbs, and nonverbal communication, rapport, and trust in the physician-patient relationship as key concepts. Coaching in Health Care is designed to address this competency and equip physicians with the skills necessary to be successful.

In health care, wherever there is a need or an opportunity to build teams, problem-solve in adaptive situations, mentor learners, such as medical students, or invite others to share their thinking, there is a place for this coaching series.

Coaching in Health Care is an eighteen-hour webinar delivered over two to four months. Two beta groups were conducted with physicians and surgeons in the spring of 2021. Subsequently, the course was accredited by the Royal College of Physicians and Surgeons of Canada. It has since been offered six more times between 2021 and 2024. One group was comprised of surgeons in Quebec and was presented in French and English and was funded for research by the Royal College of Physicians and Surgeons of Canada. This version was subtitled Coaching for Wellness and was designed to study the impact of the integration of coaching skills on levels of burnout. The results, soon to be published, showed a positive impact on physician wellness and a reduction of burnout levels as measured by the Maslach Burnout Inventory. The qualitative interviews revealed that the reductions in burnout were due to the greater sense of efficacy with patients with complex issues, a reduction in anxiety to "have solutions," and a greater connection with patients and others. Through a personalized learning approach that provided intention to the skills of listening, paraphrasing, and offering questions, physicians found that they had a greater capacity to engage with patients and situations with empathy, compassion, and authentic engagement (Daniels et al. manuscript in publication, 2024). This model continues to be refined and to be in demand.

> *No one likes feeling helpless. But by turning toward such uncomfortable feelings, rather than shutting them down, I become more effective as a doctor and feel more alive as a human being.* (Dr. Ronald Epstein, *Attending: Medicine, Mindfulness and Humanity*. Simon and Schuster, 2017, New York)

In October 2021, this Cognitive Coaching emerged in the United States health sector through WakeMed Hospitals and Health in Raleigh, North Carolina. The Cognitive Coaching Foundation Seminar was offered. The first cohort consisted of surgical and specialty divisional heads, organizational leads in counseling, human resources, social work, and nursing. Engagement was palpable, and contributions to the learning experience and applications to daily work were shared by all participants. Consequently, there are now three internal Cognitive Coaching trainers providing this work to that organization. WakeMed offered eight Foundation Seminars between October 2021 and May 2024. Here are some of the testimonials regarding the impact of this learning experience:

Dr. Harr (chief medical officer and surgeon–WakeMed): *Cognitive Coaching is a method of listening effectively and empowering an individual to reach insightful and intuitive decisions concerning challenges they are faced with.* Dr. Harr is also a rear admiral (RET), US Navy chief medical officer who trained field surgeons in Desert Storm whom, he acknowledged, needed to be self-directed.

Dr. Theresa Amerson, physician and chief medical officer (Population Health), was the subject of a video presented to the WakeMed Board of Directors. Dr. Amerson discussed her applications of her learning in the Cognitive Coaching Seminar. She provided two examples of how her coaching skills were appropriate, applicable, and valuable:

1. the colleague that wanted my opinion and advice, instead of offering advice I put some of the skills I had learned in Cognitive Coaching into play. I was able to listen in a different way. By pausing and paraphrasing to reflect back to that colleague what I was hearing her say, I was able to clarify her thinking. The colleague came up with a really great solution on her own and one that I wouldn't have been able to come up with. The colleague also remarked that it was the most helpful seven minutes in her day.

2. I was working with a patient who was struggling with a screening recommendation presented to her. Prior to this training I would have reiterated the need for the screening. It turns out that this patient was afraid of needles so (I paraphrased that) she really wanted to feel safe but also wanted to get this done.

The patient felt heard and ended up taking the screening. I felt more satisfied with this interaction. Dr. Amerson's recommendation is that we

> incorporate this style of communication in everything we do. It would be important for us to connect back to the art of medicine. To deal with people as people . . . putting their needs first . . . and create a safe place to offer our expertise. To validate each other's perspectives.

In survey information from 126 WakeMed Foundation Seminar participants, the majority of participants identified the benefit of valuing the coachee's ability to solve their own issues or rely on their own resources and not fixing or solving. This sample included twelve physicians, including five chief medical officers, multiple health professionals from finance, marketing, administration, quality improvement, diversity, and seven other departments.

In one report from twenty-seven participants, eighteen people specifically identified prioritizing "self-directedness" for the coachee as a key strength of the Cognitive Coaching model. All participants highlighted the skills of rapport, listening, and paraphrasing as professionally relevant and powerful relational skills.

WakeMed represents an example of a health care setting which has confirmed the credibility and utility of the model and contributed to the impetus for adaptivity and expansion to and growth within other sectors as well.

Recommendations

The universality of learning and the intention to support, clarify, explore, and resource the thinking of others is central to many fields. Costa and Garmston maintain that Cognitive Coaching is a model of human interaction that draws on basic human skills of listening, empathy, questioning, and inquiring to improve the quality of those interactions.

Doctors, through their training, have been on a dense learning journey focused on the acquisition of knowledge and medical procedural information and expertise. If they have strong people skills, it may be more likely a function of the individual than the process. However, many doctors have identified the value of the skills of coaching while also admitting to the challenge of switching from expert to facilitator of thinking. What we have seen is that they can do it. What we have learned is that the principles of adult learning theory are particularly relevant. Adult learning theory (Kegan) identifies the elements that create powerful and lasting learning experiences for older students.

Our planning, presentation, and contextualization of this work in the health care seminars was informed by the following guidelines:

- It needs to be relatable to their context.
- It needs to be practical and immediately applicable.
- It needs to be a complement, a refinable addition to their identity.
- It needs to be seen as a "living intention to make them a better version of themselves."
- It needs to be seen as valuable and doable.

The applicability and significant value that health care professionals, including physicians, find when they action the intention and skills of coaching in their work settings has been extremely powerful. In the training, presenters have constantly provided and elicited examples of where a coaching role is appropriate and preferred to affirm the coachee's experience, perspectives, and challenges. When the person being coached is a patient, the rapport and the acknowledgment and endorsement of the patient's reality are impactful.

> Turn toward suffering, not away. Listen deeply so that you can know and accompany the patient and help the patient feel understood. The novelist Henry James calls it placing an "empty cup of attention" between yourself and the patient. (Dr. Ronald Epstein, *Attending*)

The goal of Cognitive Coaching, in the beginning, was to improve the product of teaching. Similarly, the intention is also to support the thinking of anyone who is in the process of learning and growing. The goal is to broaden the principle of valuing self-directedness to any professional learning context. We need to meet them where they are and "who they are." "Cognitive Coaching is intended to support individuals in increasing the complexity and usefulness of their thinking leading to elevated efficacy and action" (Costa).

There is a need to adapt the model to accommodate the setting. It can be done, and it has been done with significant success. There is a need for health care professionals to make the shift from an expert on how an individual or team can be or do better to a humble supporter of the thinking of another or of others.

Costa and Garmston believe that it is important to preserve and protect the fundamental principles, values, and beliefs of the original model of Cognitive Coaching. However, moving forward, they also advise that the model must be adaptive. The configuration of the content and delivery, the platform of presentation, the inclusion of established and evolving research, and the present model for the development of qualified trainers must all be evaluated and adapted to respond to the growing need and interest in Cognitive Coaching. We need to make this work more accessible to health care professionals.

Accessibility in health care means the following:

- The coaching model is designed to support the clinical encounter as a central component, with the opportunity for providers to fund additional contextual applications.
- It holds the identity of the provider as central, and additional skills complement and refine the professional identity.
- The design is rooted in and taught with reference to scientific evidence and evidence-based practice.
- It is offered in "bite-sized" components that do not interfere with clinical practice.
- It is rooted in what they already know but stretches their comfort over time.

Many medical bodies and health care organizations share a lack of clarity about what coaching actually is. We have provided that clarity through our delivery of both Cognitive Coaching Seminars and Coaching in Health Care.

Thanks to Dr. Arthur Costa and Dr. Robert Garmston, Cognitive Coaching was designed for learners, thinkers, and servers. This model of human communication has the potential to enhance the quality of all professional conversations. It is the way in which individuals can live and work humanely with each other.

References

CanMEDS Physician Competencies Framework. (2015). *CanMEDS Physician Competencies Framework.*
Costa, A. L., & Garmston, R. J. (2016). *Cognitive Coaching: A foundation for renaissance schools* (3rd ed.). Rowman & Littlefield.
Ellison, J., & Hayes, C. (2003). *John Dyer: Cognitive coaching in business and industry.* Christopher-Gordon.
Epstein, R. (2017). *Attending: Medicine, mindfulness, and humanity.* Simon and Schuster.
Sills-Maerov, M. (2019). Cognitive coaching: A leadership essential? *Canadian Journal of Physician Leadership, 6*(2).

Coaching and Teaching Vocal Music

Sue Pressler

10

Preparing Students for Performance (p. 97)

Understanding How Music Influences Focus and Mood (p. 100)

Conclusion (p. 101)

Music, be it vocal or instrumental, is best known as a performing art. However, people who truly understand music also know that to perform or understand music deeply, it is also a *thinking* art. Music teachers support students in their performance abilities, their critical thinking, and their self-direction, enabling them to become thoughtful and intentional consumers of music who understand its emotional and mental impact. This chapter will explore the role of Cognitive Coaching and music education. Two specific intentions of music teachers are to prepare students for performance and to teach students how music influences focus and mood.

Preparing Students for Performance

Preparing my students for a performance was a large part of my role as a music teacher and one I took very seriously. Even though music teachers realize that most of their students will not go on to perform music on a regular basis, it was part of my job to teach and model for my students how to prepare each piece of music on a given program. This preparation required thinking about several aspects of the music and taught my students many different skills that supported them throughout life.

Before sight-reading a piece of music, the choir would look at the music and respond to several questions. When was the piece written? How might the time it was written affect how the song should be sung? Who composed the music? What influenced the composer to write the music in that way?

After getting an understanding about the history of the music itself and the influences on the composer, we would shift to the actual music itself. When doing so, the choir would look at rhythm patterns, tempo, and the dynamics of the music. We would then discuss questions such as "What effect might suddenly shifting to *forte* immediately after singing *piano* have on the listener?" "How might performing a section *ritardando* rather than a sudden shift from *vivace* to *andante* have on the listener?" "What might be some of the reasons the composer decided to have this section be *pianissimo* rather than *piano*?" "What might be the impact on the audience if this section was sung *forte* rather than *fortissimo*?" And while looking at the tempo markings provided by the composer, "How do these tempo markings enhance the music itself and the message the music is trying to portray to the listener?" Asking these questions prior to rehearsing the piece for the first time ultimately enhanced the learning and performing of the piece of music.

Using the Planning Conversation from Cognitive Coaching, each of my rehearsals followed a similar pattern. First, clear goals were set for the rehearsal. Given our rehearsal the previous day, what goals might we have for today? Knowing we have four more rehearsals, what must we perfect today? These goals were specific and achievable for the rehearsal time. For success indicators, I would ask what the choir thought they were doing well with the selection and where they wanted to be with the song given the rhythms, dynamics, tempo, and so on. We asked ourselves questions such as What is our goal in performing this piece of music? What will we be paying attention to as we rehearse today, and What will we focus on as the soprano section? I would ask the class what they needed to bring to the rehearsal so that we might leave feeling accomplished and moving toward our performance. Throughout the rehearsal, we would continuously monitor our practice. We focused our attention on our actions and sound. We answered the question "How did we know we were accomplishing the sound, message, tone we wanted with the music?" We noticed when we were struggling with certain passages or tempos, and we asked ourselves why that might be happening. We also paid attention to how we were feeling as we sang the piece: Were we reflecting in our singing how we wanted our audience to feel?

Occasionally during rehearsal, I would ask my students to use self-questioning. They would ask themselves questions like: Why am I having difficulty with this section of the music? What do I specifically need to work on as a member of this choir to make our performance the best it can be? How will I/we listen to ensure we are blending our voices together and that not one section or voice overpowers the other voices in the choir? Given that this rhythm pattern must be precise and staccato, what might we tell ourselves as we approach this section? Additional questions we might include: How might the phrasing add to the effect the music will have on the listener? How do the dynamics of a piece support the message the piece is trying to send? In what ways do the rhythms contribute to the overall mood of the piece? Or, if the piece of music was a vocal piece: How important is the enunciation of the lyrics to the overall mood? If the song was in a foreign language, what are the nuances of that language and are we accomplishing nuances of the language?

At the end of each rehearsal, I would have the choir reflect on the practice. Using the regions of the reflective conversation, I would have them think about their collective practice as a whole choir, as well as their individual contribution to the practice. How did they feel individually/collectively about the rehearsal? What specifically were they remembering to lead them to that feeling? What did each student individually do to contribute to that feeling? How did the rehearsal compare to the rehearsal yesterday? What are we learning about ourselves as a choir? Given those learnings, what might we revisit at the next rehearsal.

We used reflective conversation after a performance as well: As most music teachers, I would record our performance, and as we watched it later, I would ask the students to think of more questions to ask. We would pause the recording throughout to have conversations. In the end, our choir kept getting better and better.

On the day of the performance, students would practice singing challenging songs or parts of songs in their heads, flawlessly and with confidence and emotion. This helped build confidence and mental readiness for the performance itself. This was a fail-proof practice that supported my students in performing their best. By incorporating metacognitive strategies, such as the questions listed throughout the rehearsal routine, students were able to enhance their awareness, self-regulation, and effectiveness as musicians. These skills would also serve them in other academic areas and in life. By thinking critically about their practice process and learning from their experiences, they were better equipped to prepare for and perform their musical selections with confidence and skill.

Understanding How Music Influences Focus and Mood

Performance is not the only goal of a music teacher. It is also important to teach students how to know and appreciate many kinds of music. My hope was they would take the knowledge, appreciation, and understanding learned about music into their adult lives. Without exposure to different types of music and the opportunity to think about what the music did for their feelings and/or thinking, many would turn on the radio and listen to the Top 40 hits or a specific genre that appealed to them without thinking deeply. Students in my classroom were intentionally exposed to all different genres of music. It was my intention that by experiencing new styles of music, they might recognize some of those elements in their favorite songs. After listening or performing, the students were always asked, "How did this music make you feel?" "What does this type of music make you think about?" "What did you like most about this music?"

Students also learned how music is created. One year, while teaching first-grade students, I developed and taught a unit about opera music, including lessons on how composers wrote operas and what were composers trying to tell when they wrote an opera, and so on. Through this teaching, I incorporated knowledge of high-level vocabulary such as arias, recitative, libretto, obbligato, and more. The students decided to turn the picture book *Stone Soup* into their very own opera. Since they knew the story very well, the students decided upon the tempo and dynamics of the opera, as well as whether the characters should sing an aria, a recitative, or something else. They also decided what the lyrics and the music should portray at different points of the storyline. The final Stone Soup Opera was created through many invitational questions and collaboration among the entire class.

As a music teacher, I knew that different genres of music could create conducive environments for concentration, deep thinking, and even stress relief. I knew that teaching students about how different music affects their focus and thinking would support them in learning in other classes. Neuroimaging research shows that music engages brain areas involved in paying attention, making predictions, and updating events in memory. Music can also have a positive effect on one's mental state. It has been proven to improve mood and increase positive emotions, reduce anxiety, and promote a more positive mindset.

There is also research that suggests different music has a direct effect on the mind and body. A few of the physiological changes that can occur when listening to slower tempo of music are reduced heart rate and blood pressure, decreased levels of the stress hormone cortisol, relaxation of muscles, and synchronized brain waves with the music's tempo. Optimal music for stress relief indicates that slower tempos around 60 beats per minute, such as classical music, particularly the "largo" movement, can induce a relaxed state. Native American, Celtic, and Indian stringed-instrument music, as well as nature sounds mixed with light jazz, can also be very effective. Knowing this information taught my students to choose the music that would best support them in accomplishing the mood or task that was needed. I taught lessons where students were asked to listen to different types of music and then share what effects those different types of music had on their concentration, their ability to focus, and/or their mood.

Conclusion

A music teacher acts as a mediator of thinking with her students by teaching them about the influences music might have on their life and the ways in which they might approach performing a selection of music. It is my hope that the many students I had the privilege to influence during my life as a music teacher have taken the knowledge learned in music class into their life as an adult listening to and performing music.

Elevating Learning
Merging Education and Business Practices

William Sommers

Efficacy as Leadership (p. 105)

States of Mind (p. 106)

Flexibility (p. 106)

Consciousness (p. 107)

Craftsmanship (p. 108)

Interdependence (p. 109)

Often you will hear educators say, "Business doesn't have the answer." Similarly, it is often heard from the business sector, "Educators don't have the answer." *ARGH!* Neither is one hundred percent correct; however, there is some truth on both sides. Both business and education have good processes that work depending upon the culture and leadership. The time is right to move from *either/or* thinking to a *both/and* mentality and use whatever strategies and actions produce results. This is a subject I have covered in several of my last books, using both education and business models to help sites and districts develop leadership skills at all levels. What we see here is a tyranny of the either/or belief system.[1]

> Not learning is bad, not wanting to learn is worse. (African proverb)

Donald Schon (1983) wrote about reflective thinking for several years before his book was published. He basically said there were two processes.

1. *Reflection-ON-Action*: the ability to review the results of the event
2. *Reflection-FOR-Action*: the ability to plan ahead; creating and following a plan of action

These two processes were the foundation of Cognitive Coaching: a planning conversation and a reflective conversation. It *is* possible to do this alone, but having a thinking partner (coach) can provide points of view, options for pathways to the desired results, resulting in collaboration and trust that develop between the person and their coach or learning partner.

> Life can only be understood backwards, but it must be lived forwards. (Soren Kierkegaard)

I would be remiss not to mention a third process: *Reflection-IN-Action*. This is where most of us spend the majority of our time. Working individually, in groups, managing direct reports, and managing up (like to your supervisor). See Gary Klein's work (1998) for more specific information. How do we get better at Reflection-IN-Action (aka "hot cognition")? Klein posits two suggestions based on operating room personnel, firefighters, and emergency medical technicians.

1. Pattern recognition
2. Mental simulation (this is exactly where a planning conference helps)

In Cognitive Coaching, the focus is on the internal thought processes that an individual or a thinking partner (coach) can reflect on and take action toward—the future instructional and leadership strategies. One of the key learnings from the 1980s, when Cognitive Coaching was being developed and refined, was that coaches needed to model what they were expecting individuals and teams to do, therefore elevating their own thinking processes.

> Children need models more than critics. (French proverb)

Strategic questioning is one of the most used skills in Cognitive Coaching and in most models. Several business sources expand my and other coaches' skills. Peter Block (2002) in his book *The Answer to How Is Yes* provides many questions and examples on how to build community and participation.

Here is an example of some effective reframing questions:

- Question: "How long is this going to take?"
- Reframe: "If this is important, how much time are we willing to spend on it?"

Block's bonus question is one I often use in coaching leaders: "What question, if you had the answer to, would set you free?" In coaching, I use the stem, "What question, if you had the answer to ___?" Team learning? Leadership team development? Student learning? Complete with your own specific content!

Another excellent source is Edgar Schein and Peter Schein (2021) *Humble Inquiry*. Schein defines this as "the fine art of drawing someone out, of asking questions to which you do not already know the answer, of building a relationship based on curiosity and interest in the other person." Humble Inquiry can open up curiosity about how individuals and systems work. There are many examples in his book, which help move from the culture of "tell" to the culture of curiosity.

> The leader of the past knew how to tell, but the leader of the future will know how to ask. (Peter Drucker)

Efficacy as Leadership

The research literature is filled with references to efficacy for teachers, students, leaders, and teams. The higher the efficacy, the more positive are the results. Marshall Goldsmith, the number one business coach for ten years in a row, says the team or organization never got better because of him. The leader or team are the ones doing the work. As a certified Stakeholder Centered Coach in Goldsmith's organization, I have seen educational leaders develop efficacy at higher levels because of their actions and the resulting effects on staff members.

Goldsmith coined the term "FeedForward." We can learn from feedback on how a process worked and in a reflective conference decide what to keep doing and what to jettison in favor of another approach. Think about it. There is nothing you can do after the fact. (A quick caveat: If you have injured someone with words or deeds, then by all means, make amends and do what you can to correct the situation!) FeedForward is a process to build more efficacy in what you will do in the future. Efficacy means you can and will take responsibility for your future actions because you *believe* you can make a difference.

In Goldsmith's model, a leader, teacher, and others, chooses people they trust to be stakeholders. These are people who are receiving the leadership or teaching from the client/employee/direct report. (We are currently using this model with students.) Get feedback from the stakeholders, choose one or two goals, coach around those goals, and assess midcourse and at the end of the coaching. He saw 95 percent positive results based on over 90,000 leaders in business and 90 percent with educational leaders.

This, of course, is key for student success as well. See Jon Saphier's book (2017) *High Expectations Teaching* for fifty practical ways staff and leaders can implement to help students believe they are talented learners.

States of Mind

Cognitive Coaching skills prepared me for conversations around the "States of Mind" and are extremely important for producing growth for both the leader and the coach. Taking a page from Edgar Scheins's work (2009) *Helping*, it is important to level the relationship. Not one up and one down but, as Art Costa has said, co-cognition. Trust is a major goal of Cognitive Coaching.

> People's beliefs about their abilities have a profound effect on those abilities. (Albert Bandura)

One of the most important foundational tenets from the early days of creating Cognitive Coaching was the creation of States of Mind, which will be used as an organizer for this chapter with support from the business literature. These were introduced earlier in this book, but as a quick refresher, the States of Mind are:

- Flexibility
- Consciousness
- Craftsmanship
- Interdependence

Flexibility

A company like Pixar is very creative. They are focused on finding problems with stories, films, or production which are not as good as they could be and finding ways to make them better. In Ed Catmull's book (2014) *Creativity*, he presents Pixar's process of the BrainTrust. This takes "psychological safety" that Amy Edmondson (2019) writes about. In her book, she has six or seven questions that give an indication of how flexible and safe the organization is in producing creative solutions to problems.

In Cognitive Coaching, a coach helps create options for the person you are coaching to implement. Edgar Schein wrote that if you must suggest something, at least suggest two things and let the person you are coaching choose which one best suits them. It is their choice, not the coach's. Personally, I recommend three. I heard Art and Bob at one of our meetings say, "The person with the most flexibility has the most influence in the conversation." That was a good message. I also use the acronym STAR (Save Time, Add Repertoire).

On a side note: You may think *outside* the box, but you must work *inside* the box. No business or educational organization I know of can replace all employees or have unlimited funds to change the system. (Get real.) I wrote about this in *Creating Talent Density* (2021). DARPA has a saying: "When faced with a challenge, get smarter." Find alternative pathways to solve issues and create options for action. One size usually fits one; there are always nuances. As a high school principal, I know that there is no rule or policy that can't be beaten. Students taught me that. There are always adaptations. As Goldsmith's book title suggests, "What got you here won't get you there."

This is why flexibility in thinking is so important and one of the foundational elements of Cognitive Coaching. The most innovative companies today are not looking for high SAT scores, GPAs, or even degrees. They want someone who can contribute to the mission of the company. Again, psychological safety encourages flexibility in thinking and trying solutions to problems without fear of negative repercussions.

Where all think alike, no one thinks very much. (Walter Lippmann)

Consciousness

What are you aware of? That will determine what a person focuses on. The quality of life and the quality of your work depend upon what you pay attention to. Brain research confirms a few basics:

1. There is NO such thing as multitasking. Multi-switching, yes, but one can only pay attention to one thing at a time.

2. To mediate a person's thinking, the subject or goal must be in the "working memory." A coach sometimes must help the learning partner surface the topic at hand.
3. George Miller's research confirms there is a limited amount of space for concepts. He referred to the "magic number 7" and theorized that the brain can only pay attention to seven items, plus or minus two depending on a person's stress level. A coach, therefore, must keep the issue in the coachee's attention.

Several years ago, a cognitive coach was working on her dissertation and interviewed Dr. Peter Senge, author of *The 5th Discipline*. When asked which one of the State of Mind was the most important, Senge said, "consciousness." When she asked why that was the most important, Senge replied, "If you are not conscious of an issue, nothing else makes sense." A powerful answer that supports having a topic in your working memory to be able to process an issue.

Cognitive Coaching offers language cues to help this by embedding presuppositions, intonation, syntax, and response strategies to encourage deeper thought. Positive presuppositions are key to assuming positive intention and putting the coachee in the best possible thinking state.

> *In a lifetime you will pay attention to about 185 billion bits of information.*
>
> *The type of 185 billion bits of information we let into our consciousness determines the quality of life we experience.* (Mihaly Csikszentmihalyi)

Craftsmanship

What coaching really means is that improvement is everyone's responsibility. How do we get better? Deming said, "Quality comes not from inspection but from improvement of the process." His first tenet is to drive out fear (psychological safety keeps coming back). Trust, learning, and self-direction are three main goals of Cognitive Coaching.

To improve, a new approach required supervisors to be coaches and counselors, not micromanagers. One of Richard Sheridan's motto at Menlo Innovations (Joy, Inc. 2013) is "Run the experiment." Essentially, try it and see if it works. Then, I use the "Reverse Las Vegas Effect": If it works, tell everybody. If it doesn't work, tell everybody. Save time by spreading the learning throughout the system.

Sheridan has developed one of the best learning strategies I have seen. It is called "Hey Menlo." The forty-five to fifty people working in the office meet standing in a circle. Two-member teams grab one side of a Vikings helmet and answer three questions:

1. What are we working on?
2. What are we learning?
3. Where might we need help?

This takes about fifteen to twenty minutes. People help each other, have conversations about the work they're doing, and share their learnings. It is an amazing thing that Art and I have witnessed; they get more learning in a short amount of time to make continual improvement.

Craftsmanship comes from the total quality management (TQM) process Deming led for several companies. Drive out fear; leaders are 85 percent responsible for what goes on, with 15 percent from employees. We should focus on what we can do to improve. As you can tell, this is how the set of States of Mind intends to positively affect systems. It is no longer about content acquisition in individuals, but rather the process of learning, transferring the learning to others in the organizations and transforming systems to keep on learning.

When parents or community say the learning in schools was good enough for them and will be good enough for their kids, *they are wrong*. Learning keeps evolving as we learn new things and invent new ways to learn. Technology is not going to stop anytime soon—or ever. So, let's keep getting better, assessing how we are doing, and learning new ways to adapt to an ever-changing world.

If you don't like change, you will like irrelevance a lot less. (General Erik Shinseki)

Interdependence

The States of Mind listed previously can be done individually, but *interdependence* is a team sport. James Suroweicki (2004) in his book *Wisdom of Crowds* quotes research that shows the positive outcomes of the smartest individual in a group are 65 percent. When the group creates solutions, the effectiveness is 91 percent. More people, more perspectives, and better decisions. So, when coaching an individual, who do they go to for suggestions? Who do they trust?

Sally Helgesen (2018), the premier authority on women in leadership, writes that stereotypes prevent women and people of color from contributing their perspective when the team doesn't create the conditions for volunteering their point of view. She says, "People in organizations often assign one another roles based on previous behavior, which has the effect of making it difficult to practice new ones."

In her book titled *Inclusify*, Stephanie Johnson (2020) suggests that coaching teams is beneficial for opening up communication, collegiality, and confidence in being more inclusive in addition to making better decisions. None of us can do hard work alone.

> Give a good idea to a mediocre team, and they will screw it up.
>
> Give a mediocre idea to a great team, and they will either fix it or come up with something better.
>
> If you get the team right, chances are that they'll get the ideas right. (Ed Catmull)

As Goldsmith (2007) states, the best clients who get the most out of coaching have three qualities:

1. Courage to confront real data
2. Humility to admit they could increase their skill set
3. Discipline to follow through

Promoting all three in organizations will benefit individuals, teams, and the organizations they work, no matter the vocation.

> It takes courage to admit that you have been doing something wrong, to admit that you have something to learn, that there is a better way. (Edwards Deming)

My suggestion: Get a coach, have regular learning conversations, and develop a cadre of thinking partners who will support, challenge, and add to your repertoire of skills.

In conclusion: *Learn everywhere you can, from whoever you can, at any time you can.* Richard Sheridan also says, "Leaders are Readers." Read and experience outside your own system. There is a world waiting for you. And as Art so eloquently says, "Make learning happen."

Note

1 See https://learningomnivores.com/rules/the-tyranny-of-or/ for more specifics.

References

Block, P. (2002). *The answer to how is yes*. Berrett-Koehler.
Catmull, E. (2014). *Creativity, Inc*. Random House.
Edmondson, A. (2019). *The fearless organization*. John Wiley & Sons.
Goldsmith, M. (2007). *What got you here won't get you there*. Hyperion.
Helgesen, S., & Goldsmith, M. (2018). *How women rise*. Hachette Books.
Johnson, S. (2020). *Inclusify*. HarperCollins.
Klein, G. (1998). *Sources of power: How people make decisions*. The MIT Press.
Saphier, J. (2017). *High expectations teaching*. Corwin Press.
Schein, E. (2009). *Helping: How to offer, give, and receive help*. Berrett-Koehler Publishers, Inc.
Schein, E. (2013). *Humble inquiry: The gentle art of asking instead of telling*. Berrett-Koehler. Inc.
Schein, E. H., & Schein, P. A. (2025). *Humble inquiry: The gentle art of asking instead of telling*. Berrett-Koehler Publishers.
Schon, D. (1983). *The reflective practitioner*. Basic Books, Inc.
Surowiecki, J. (2004). *The wisdom of crowds*. Anchor Books.

Section IV

Enduring Values and Deepening Learning

Introduction

Skillful Cognitive Coaches have a tool chest of interactive behaviors. They listen with understanding and empathy, they pose questions to challenge the intellect, and they provide nonjudgmental feedback. All of these behaviors, however, have a deeper meaning and therefore an expanded intent. They are the behaviors that are needed in a community of interdependence, peace, and love—it's what the world needs now. Values, not behaviors, define the coach's work. Trust, respect, and self-directedness inform the coaches choices, each a key factor in the permanence of this work.

Cognitive Coaching in Retrospect
Why It Persists

12

The Roots of Cognitive Coaching (p. 116)
Cognitive Coaching: A Research-Based Strategy (p. 117)
What We've Learned (p. 118)
Becoming Clearer about Vision and Mission (p. 118)
Metacognitive Capabilities of a Mediator (p. 118)
Neuro-Biochemical Effects of Authentic Paraphrasing (p. 120)
We Can't Always Coach (p. 121)
Weaving Cognitive Coaching Ideals throughout the Culture (p. 122)
The Nature of Recent Changes (p. 122)
Why Cognitive Coaching Persists (p. 123)
In Summary (p. 126)

What causes an innovation to evolve into an educational staple? What is it about some supervisory and professional development practices that sustain themselves over time? What distinguishes a fad that will fade from a fresh practice that will last many seasons?

In the February 1985 issue of *Educational Leadership* (Costa & Garmston, 1985), we expressed our earliest thoughts about cognition, teaching, and supervision. We described the "invisible" cognitive processes of instruction—

what happens inside a teacher's head prior to, during, and after teaching. We suggested that changing perceptions and cognition were prerequisites to enhancing instructional behaviors, and we suggested coaching interventions intended to engage and transform teachers' thinking.

Forty years of development have occurred since that first article. Cognitive Coaching has been taught in university preparation courses for supervisors and administrators and used by thousands of teachers, administrators, and staff developers in mentoring, supervision, and professional development activities throughout the United States and around the world. At this point in its history, Cognitive Coaching is burgeoning and is an influential model for mentoring, supervision, organizational culture, staff development, and classroom instruction. What might be contributing to this rigor?

The purpose of this chapter is to reflect on what has been learned these past forty years in an effort to explain the nature of the changes as they might relate to the question of sustainability. We will first, briefly, review the uniqueness of Cognitive Coaching and its mission, report the research, and disclose our most recent insights into how Cognitive Coaching contributes to deep and permanent changes in teaching effectiveness, individuals, and school cultures. Next, we will share several possible reasons for the persistence and growth of Cognitive Coaching over nearly four decades.

But first we must acknowledge the mass below the water moving an iceberg. On the surface, we see coaching interactions, collaborative enterprises, improved relations, more effective teaching, student benefits, enhanced relationships, and a sense of purpose.

Below the water, accounting for 90 percent of an iceberg's mass is the swelling expansion of humility, humanity, and holonomy. The world becomes a humbler, more thoughtful, more nurturing, and all-around better place as a result of thousands of caring coaching conversations across the globe. At no time has this been more called for.

The Roots of Cognitive Coaching

Cognitive Coaching's early roots were drawn from the work of Morris Cogan, Robert Goldhammer, and Robert Anderson working at Harvard's Master of Arts in Teaching program in the mid-1950s. Prior to that time, supervisors did the talking and teachers did the listening. Cogan envisioned a "clinical supervision" model in which the purpose was "the development of professionally responsible teachers, who are analytic of their own performance, open to help from others and self-directing" (Cogan, 1973).

Later, Madeline Hunter borrowed the term "clinical supervision" and, using Cogan's structure (which had been conceptualized as early as 1925) of a pre-conference, observation, and post conference, modified the original practices to be more supervisor-directed (Brandt, 1985). As other approaches to supervision have been introduced, they too have been presented within the framework of clinical supervision until the term has lost its original meaning about the particular points of view and practices associated with its use. The practice of both Cogan's and Hunter's models has grown dim in recent years.

Most models, in time, expire. Pajak (2000) notes that three original clinical supervision models appeared in the 1960s to early 1970s (Goldhammer, Mosher & Purpel, and Cogan) and two Humanistic/Artistic models from mid 1970 to early 1980s (Blumberg and Eisner). From early to mid 1980s, three Technical/Didactic models appeared (Acheson & Gall, Hunter, and Joyce & Showers). From the mid 1980s to mid 1990s eight Developmental/Reflective models appeared (Glickman, Costa & Garmston, Schon, Zeichner & Liston, Garman, Smyth & Retallick, Bowers & Flinders, and Waite).

Cognitive Coaching: A Research-Based Strategy

Numerous studies have investigated the benefits of Cognitive Coaching. Five various investigations examined the influence of Cognitive Coaching on teachers' thought processes, conceptual development, and reflective thinking (Lindsey, D. B.). Other studies examined the effects on teachers' self-directed learning, efficacy, craftsmanship, consciousness, flexibility, and interdependence. Some studies investigated its effects on students, on school culture, and on the personal and professional lives of teachers. As you read previously in the chapter by Jenny Edwards in Section I of this book, studies examined the use of Cognitive Coaching in supervisory relationships, university classes, and teacher preparation programs. To summarize once more, here are eight major findings:

1. Cognitive Coaching was linked with increased student test scores and other student benefits.
2. Teachers grew in teaching efficacy.
3. Cognitive Coaching impacted teacher thinking, causing teachers to be more reflective and to think in more complex ways.
4. Teachers were more satisfied with their positions and with their choice of teaching as a profession.
5. School cultures became more professional.
6. Teachers collaborated more.

7. Cognitive Coaching assisted teachers professionally.
8. Cognitive Coaching benefited teachers personally.

What We've Learned

Over the years, with the help of a large number of associates, we've continued to grow and change. We have refined our presentation strategies, become clearer about our purposes, and more able to adroitly articulate the beliefs, values, skills, and maps basic to Cognitive Coaching.

Becoming Clearer about Vision and Mission

Originally, coaching goals were three: trust, learning, and autonomy (Costa, Garmstom, 2015). Today we regard these as necessary pathways leading to a larger mission: to produce self-directed individuals with the cognitive capacity for excellence, both independently and as members of a community. Self-directed people are described as:

- *Self-Managing*: They approach tasks with clarity of outcomes, a strategic plan, and necessary data, and then draw from past experiences, anticipate success indicators, and create alternatives for accomplishment.
- *Self-Monitoring*: They establish metacognitive strategies to alert the perceptions to in-the-moment indicators of whether the strategic plan is working and to assist in the decision-making processes of altering the plan if it is not.
- *Self-Modifying*: They reflect on, evaluate, analyze, and construct meaning from the experience and apply the learning to future activities, tasks, and challenges.

Metacognitive Capabilities of a Mediator

We've become clearer about the metacognitive skills of coaching that produce the results described above. Four capabilities, or metacognitive skills, inform a coach's moment-to-moment decisions in coaching and in other support functions. These are learnable and accelerate one's gaining effectiveness as a coach.

1. Knowing One's Intentions and Choosing Congruent Behaviors

   The ultimate goal of Cognitive Coaching is to help an individual become self-mediating. With that end in mind, coaches are clear about their intentions in the moment and consciously choose behaviors that support those intentions. This capability includes the ability to calibrate the effects of coaching behaviors.

2. Setting Aside Unproductive Patterns of Listening, Responding, and Inquiring (Costa, Garmston)

   Mediators monitor and manage their own listening skills by devoting their mental energies to the other person's verbal and nonverbal communications. To listen with such intensity requires holding in abeyance certain tempting, but unproductive, behaviors that may interfere with the ability to hear and understand a colleague:

   - *Autobiographical listening* occurs when the brain exercises its associative powers. The colleague's story stimulates us to think of our own experiences. Coaches set this type of listening aside as they become aware their attention has drifted into their own story.
   - *Inquisitive listening* occurs when we become curious about portions of the story that are not relevant to the problem at hand. Knowing what information is and is not important is a critical characteristic of Cognitive Coaching. Curiosity about that which is not relevant to the mediational moment sinks the conversation into a hole of analytical minutiae and causes coach and teacher to lose sight of the larger issues.
   - *Solution listening* is when we serve as a problem solver for another. This is appropriate when consulting but not coaching. When coaching, thinking of solution approaches as your colleague speaks interferes with understanding the situation from the colleague's perspective.

3. Adjusting One's Own Style Preferences

   Distinct patterns of perceiving and processing information transcend race and culture, are found within males and females, and are observable at all age levels. Conscious of these differences, cognitive coaches strive to be flexible communicators. They recognize their own style preferences and adjust their communication to most effectively connect with others who may operate from different cognitive styles.

4. Navigating among and within Coaching Maps and Support Functions

   Humans reference many mental maps to guide their interactions in different settings—problem-solving steps, brainstorming rules, algorithms, and other organizers for procedural knowledge. Three basic maps provide the cognitive coach with information about the functions of planning, reflecting, and problem-resolving. Coaches make decisions within and across coaching maps, such as the sequence with which elements in a planning conversation are discussed. Coaches are likewise alert to a moment during a reflecting conversation, for example, when it might be appropriate to switch to a problem-resolving conversation. In addition, clear intentions and knowing a range of support functions inform decisions about when to consult, collaborate, or coach.

Neuro-Biochemical Effects of Authentic Paraphrasing

Little change has occurred in the interactive tools used for Cognitive Coaching. The response behaviors of rapport, acknowledging, paraphrasing, clarifying, and providing data retain their importance as does questioning to mediate thinking. However, significant advancements in understanding neurological and chemical responses to authentic paraphrasing have occurred. Safety, but not comfort, is a prerequisite to reflective thought. Disequilibrium is a common gateway to learning. Even the most penetrating questions provide an ecosystem of cognitive and psychological safety when preceded by authentic paraphrasing.

How? Sensory signals from the eye and ear travel first in the brain to the thalamus. They are routed from there in two directions—with lightning speed to the amygdala, a threat detector, then if safe, to the neocortex for the more ponderous processes of thinking. Therefore, if threat, fear, or pain in even the most minute portions are perceived, neurological and chemical responses occur which prepare the system for survival, not reflection. With no threat, the input moves to the cortical regions where thinking can occur. Our current understanding is that an authentic paraphrase becomes a heroine in a neuro-biochemical drama. She releases neurotransmitters, allowing neurons to communicate more effectively; peptides, which carry 95 percent of the body's information through the bloodstream; and hormones that make the brain more efficient, metaphorically allowing access to the cognitive centers. So, when posing cognitively demanding questions about one's practice, if there is no paraphrase, there will be no thought.

Paraphrasing, it turns out, is not a language skill. It is a listening skill. In supporting reflective thinking, its three most common uses are: to clarify and acknowledge, to summarize and organize, and to lift the logical level of thought. The "I hear you saying . . ." phrase is perceived as inauthentic and dulls the potential effectiveness of reflective listening. Authentic paraphrasing increases the complexity of another person's thought, a characteristic of experts in any field.

We Can't Always Coach

Initially we were so enamored with the power of mediation that we concentrated on Cognitive Coaching as a single form of teacher support. Our position has changed. Support providers such as mentors, administrators, and supervisors need a repertoire and situational flexibility to achieve the ultimate goal of developing high-performing individuals. While there may be a few situations where a person's full-time job is to coach others, most often the coaching function is but a part of many duties. Individuals in these roles sometimes coach, sometimes consult, sometimes collaborate, and sometimes evaluate.

Initially we were unclear how a support person could shift from coaching to other forms of interaction—to consulting, collaborating, or evaluating and maintaining psychological safety. Michael Grinder's work in nonverbal aspects of communication, and Laura Lipton and Bruce Wellman's pioneering work in mentoring have helped us understand the distinctly different roles a support provider can play, how to shift functions and still have the default position be supporting self-directed learning. Today we find it essential for support providers to use and clearly distinguish between and among four categories of functions intended to support teacher development.

A cognitive coach's major responsibility is to increase the self-directedness of others. Coaches, to attain psychological safety and cognitive demand, must attend to both learning and relationships. Whether to and how to signal a deviation from coaching is a critical question for a coach. Such decisions are largely driven by the coach's attention to the verbal and nonverbal cues that reveal the teacher's thinking and feelings. The coach, reading the colleague's communication, may infer confidence, confusion, or discomfort and may thus infer the need to move to a different stance. Cognitive Coaching remains the default position to which we always return and that guides our support intentions.

Weaving Cognitive Coaching Ideals throughout the Culture

Cognitive Coaching has significantly expanded its reach in the last forty years. Our early work defined Cognitive Coaching as a formal dyadic interactive strategy, initially between a supervisor and teacher, in which the purpose was to support the teacher's cognitive development related to instructional decision-making. Today its use is often less formal, and we find that Cognitive Coaching's purposes are less likely to be restricted to those supervisory interactions of planning conversations, classroom observations, reflecting conversations, or problem-resolving dialogues. Rather, the work is also being used to improve the collaborative work cultures of schools and to imbue the goal of self-directed learning into school aims.

As the practices of Cognitive Coaching spread, its principles, beliefs, and values increasingly are being applied in everyday informal communications and at every level within the organization, regardless of role: teacher to peers, teacher to child, staff developer to teacher, educator to parent. The settings in which coaches find opportunities to mediate often present themselves spontaneously, such as during a conversation in the faculty room or in the hall or on the way to class. Neither is coaching exclusively the domain of traditional hierarchical relationships. Mentor teachers are coaching superintendents, teachers, principals, and so on.

The ideals of Cognitive Coaching—its values, beliefs, maps, and tools—are valued not only for staff but also for students and the entire organization. Many schools and districts have found that as Cognitive Coaching becomes embedded in the culture, all the inhabitants of the school community become increasingly self-directed and more resourceful, deliberate, reflective, and skillful.

The Nature of Recent Changes

The changes noted above seem to cluster in two categories. One is work below the surface of what one might see in a mediational interaction. We have worked at the heart of CC, refining our vision and mission. We have learned more about the invisible skills of coaching in such a way that four coaching capabilities are teachable and learnable by aspiring coaches. Deeper understandings of some of the neuro-biochemical patterns in coaching have provided us further insights on how to promote learning.

A second category of change is about context. On one hand, it involves learning to place Cognitive Coaching in the context of other support services for teachers. On the other hand, it includes expanding the venues in which Cognitive Coaching can be used and devising workable protocols for these new settings. Today, we see Cognitive Coaching in conversations related to teaching standards; we see it in classroom instruction, in parent conferences, in public coaching, in shaping collaborative work cultures, in informing school construction, in application in industrial settings, and in private enterprise.

What is present in both these dimensions are changes that protect the integrity, complexity, purposes, and values of the Cognitive Coaching model. What we do not see are changes that simplify by making practices less rigorous, that cosmeticize to make it more attractive to more people, that shorten to make training less arduous, nor do we see marketing to enlist more participants. CC has been a program of attraction and not of enlistment.

Why Cognitive Coaching Persists

We propose several possible reasons that might help explain why Cognitive Coaching is moving into its fifth decade of application.

1. **A unique mental model**

Differing from other models, Cognitive Coaching focuses not on behaviors but on the source of behaviors. Its intent is to mediate the invisible, internal mental resources and intellectual functions related to the teachers' goals. These resources include perceptions, cognitive processes, values, and five States of Mind as wellsprings of well-being and effective performance. Recipients often claim that Cognitive Coaching has changed their lives and speak of it with almost missionary zeal. Other forms of coaching tend to focus mostly on behaviors, the lesson, the topic, meeting, or activity.

2. **Its roots provide a firm foundation**

A second possible reason for Cognitive Coaching's sustainability is that its deep roots penetrate the rich soil of academic excellence in a variety of diverse but related disciplines.

3. **Adaptivity**

A third reason for Cognitive Coaching's continued growth might be its adaptivity to new knowledge, lessons from practice, and developments in related disciplines. Adaptivity implies changing form but maintaining or clarifying identity. So throughout its history of modifications, values have been maintained, goals refined, and a commitment to human potential realized. Guided by these developmental principles, training designs have evolved, the Cognitive Coaching process refined, and dozens of research studies of its effectiveness conducted; advances in the neurosciences both illuminate the reasons for its effectiveness and guide continuing refinements. Finally, the weight of learning and development has been so strong because its processes involve many people. Communities of learning were formed, expanded, and reformed many times over the course of our history. To these dedicated people, Cognitive Coaching owes its resilience today.

4. A philosophical haven in the greater culture

A fourth possible dynamic for sustainability is related to the context in which an educational practice exists. At the time Cognitive Coaching was introduced in 1985, the dominant orientation in supervision practices was behavioral, focusing on popularized generalizations about effective teaching practices. Cognitive Coaching represented an alternative, focusing on the cognitive sciences and was valued by some educators, we believe, precisely because it reflected a point of view of adult learning largely absent in the practices of the time.

The early principles and values of Cognitive Coaching have remained constant, foreshadowing current orientations toward teaching and learning. Yet, today's educational context is schizophrenic in several respects. On one hand, there is an emphasis on reflective practice not present in the mid-1980s. Constructivist learning patterns emphasize student goal-setting, self-reflection, and self-improvement. Staff development, mentoring, and supervisory practices expound, and in many cases deliver, developmentally sound work in reflective dialogue around instruction. But at the same time, schools face what Fullan terms a sea of excessive, inconsistent, relentless demands. For the first time in education history, teacher, administrator, school, and district approval is being linked to student performance rather than compliance to regulations. Accountability practices are emerging in virtually every state based on external standards for student learning, assessments based on those standards, and either sanction provisions for "educationally bankrupt" districts and at a minimum public humiliation through the publication of test scores for those schools that do not live up to political expectations for improvement. Content standards for student learning have become so prominent that, by one account, if teachers were to spend just thirty minutes on each benchmark in standards documents, another six years of schooling would be needed.

Cognitive Coaching is a fountain of cool water in a parched landscape. The continuing strength of Cognitive Coaching as a model of professional development may be that in this period of unremitting pressure on teachers and administrators, the heart seeks what is sound, the mind, once engaged, will entertain to the degree possible reflective practices as best it can achieve them.

5. **Creating an essential resource for school improvement**

A forty-year collection of both quantitative and qualitative research on school-community change and its impact on student learning demonstrates that the quality of school relationships operating in and around schools is central to their functioning and strongly predicts student outcomes. This is consistent with other studies but goes further in making specific linkages to student achievement. Relational trust, this study reveals, is essential but not sufficient for school improvement. Schools with little or no relational trust have little chance of improving. Matching teacher survey data with scores of the 100 Chicago schools that made the greatest gains on standardized tests of math and reading between 1991 and 1996, they found that schools with a high level of trust at the outset had a 1 in 2 chance of making significant improvements in math and reading. Schools with weak trust relationships had only a 1 in 7 chance of making gains, and the only ones that did gain strengthened trust over a period of years. Not only is trust a basic premise in Cognitive Coaching itself, it communicates positive regard, demonstrates respect, builds competence, and is based on integrity, the four contributing factors to relational trust. Furthermore, the social organization of schooling imposes distinct role relationships upon the different sets of school inhabitants. Particular expectations and obligations characterize each role in teacher-to-teacher interactions, teachers to parents, teachers to administrators, and administrators to parents. Each is dependent on and to an extent vulnerable to the other. To work together harmoniously, communication skills, and above all, authentic listening are musts.

Would Cognitive Coaching have persisted if no benefits to the social fabric of the school accrued? We think, possibly not. Innovation persistence may depend, in part, on collateral benefits. When what occurs between a principal and a teacher in private conversations can have an effect on others' perceptions of administrative trustworthiness, on the supportive nature of the environment, and the commitment to children's needs, it seems bound to be protected and nurtured within that system.

6. **Fulfilling an identity**

Many "closeted" reflective practitioners have admitted to us that they yearned for more liberating, holistic, and humanistic supervisory practices than those they were employing. They found that Cognitive Coaching fulfilled their "identity" as a mediator of others' inner resources. Many who embraced Cognitive Coaching reported that they felt renewed in their profession and were acting as an educator again, not a compliance technician.

Ralph Waldo Emerson is quoted as saying, "The mind, once stretched by a new idea, never returns to its original dimension." We believe this to be true for those who have experienced the reciprocally powerful relationships of Cognitive Coaching or other mediation interactions. Having been coached, one seeks it. Having coached, one values it.

In Summary

The long-range goal of Cognitive Coaching is acquiring the habits and dispositions of self-directed learning and the automation of the intellectual capacities of effective thinking. We believe that all human beings can continue growing intellectually and become increasingly self-modifying, self-referencing, and self-renewing. In this way, the intellectual functions and mental processes of effective teaching become internalized. Cognitive coaches support people in becoming self-directed autonomous agents and self-directed members of a group. These goals may be the deepest reason it prevails. Our aspirations have universal applicability, touch the personal self and professional self, are uplifting, optimistic, and freeing.

The learning journey about Cognitive Coaching and its effects are not complete. Knowledge in the field continues to expand. Challenges persist. Transformation for individuals and educational organizations remains a daunting and complex proposition. To build common vision and liberate each person's self-directedness takes time, wisdom, and skills of dedicated professionals. Indeed, as a result of forty years of experience, we now seem better able to ask more valuable and penetrating questions.

References

Brandt, R. (1985, February). On Teaching and Supervising: A Conversation with Madeline Hunter. *Educational Leadership, 42*(5), 61–66.

Costa, A., & Garmston, R. (1985, February). Supervision for intelligent teaching. *Educational Leadership, 42*(5), 70–80.

Costa, A. L., & Garmston, R. J. (2015). *Cognitive coaching: Developing self-directed leaders and learners* (Christopher-Gordon New Editions). Bloomsbury Publishing PLC.

Cogan, M. (1973). *Clinical supervision.* Houghton Mifflin Co.
Lindsey, D. *Education consultant for equity and access, and culturally proficient practices.* Author and Speaker.
Lipton & Wellman, B. Quotes 2001". Mentoring matters. Guilford, CT.
Pajak, E. (2000). *Approaches to clinical supervision: Alternatives for improving instruction.* Christopher Gordon.

"Thinking Makes It So"
Students as the Authors of Their Life Script

Laura Lipton and Steve Jambor

Developing Efficacy: Scaffolding Positive Self-Talk (p. 130)
Guilt, Grief 'n Grievance Psychology: D-Mental Block (p. 131)
D-Tailing D-Mental Block (p. 132)
D-manding (p. 133)
D-ualizing (p. 133)
Drasticating (aka Emotional Dis-regulation, Extremizing, and Dramatizing) (p. 134)
D-monizing (p. 134)
The Dialectical Dialogue: From Surface Structure to Deep Structure (p. 135)
A Dialectical Dialogue with DeeDee (p. 136)
Toward Self-Directed Learning (p. 137)

> Whether you think you can or think you can't—you're right.
> —*Henry Ford*

The relationship between self-efficacy and student achievement has been well documented (Richard et al., 2006). Efficacy refers to the belief in the ability to achieve a goal or succeed at a challenging task because you can reliably manage how you think, act, and feel. Efficacy reflects confidence in your ability to exert control over your motivation, behavior, and social environment (Bandura, 1977, 1997). Students with high levels of efficacy are better able to self-modulate, adopt a growth mindset, and have a stronger sense of agency.

How might schools operate if developing efficacy was the focus? We believe this shift would include supporting students in:

- increasing consciousness of their internal dialogue as a signaling system;
- applying a systematic approach to assessing and redirecting their own self-talk when needed; and
- scaffolding more efficacious mindsets by teaching and modeling self-directed inquiry.

This chapter describes a Cognitive Coaching approach to the development of self-efficacy, specific impediments to its development, and a structure for dialogue and reasoning to help students access the internal resources necessary for successfully navigating the world. It is an invitation to invest in growth as adults and students—and to help students exercise empowerment, agency, and voice.

Developing Efficacy: Scaffolding Positive Self-Talk

We are always in the middle of a conversation with ourselves where we author what Alfred Adler calls our life script. This expression of our creative self forms a narrative that guides our actions. This self-talk can be healthy or unhealthy. That is, it can stimulate positive and adaptive action or be undermined by faulty cognitions and fictional finalism. Efficacious students tackle problems rather than avoid them, take responsibility, bring previous success to bear on present issues and problems, and are open-minded to different perspectives. Their self-talk includes phrases like "I've got this," "This is my responsibility," and "I've succeeded before, I can do it again." They are conscious, flexible, and interdependent. These states of mind (Costa & Garmston, 2015) both develop self-efficacy and are enhanced by it creating a powerful feedback loop.

Less efficacious students are prone to defensiveness, blame, self-centeredness, and histrionics. Their self-talk sounds more like "I want this now," "It's not my fault," "It's my way or no way," or "My life is ruined if . . ."

From a social-cognitive perspective (Bandura, 1997), our actions are tempered by how we interpret the feedback from the environment. How we make sense of this social context determines the internal dialogue that shapes our sense of being in the world. The narrative that we establish will be more or less efficacious as a result. Students can be taught to pay attention and assess what they are telling themselves, determine if it is "helping or hurting" them, and to pause, breathe, and potentially reset—or continue. It's important for students to know that they are the authors of their own story, that it is fluid and changeable. You don't want a life *script* to become a life *sentence*.

Our cognition is couched in a social framework. In any group, while each member might want to proceed as the protagonist, there is the need to function in community. In negotiating this social contract, being conscious of the tension between independence and cooperation establishes our place in the I/we balance. Efficacious students search for options, create possibilities, and consider compromises. Less efficacious learners often engage in faulty cognition (see Figure 13.1).

Consider the following example:

Imagine a young girl—let's call her DeeDee—who wants to be the pitcher on her neighborhood softball team. The coach has chosen a different team member. In this scenario, DeeDee can choose to do one of several things: she can simply stand there making demands to be the pitcher; she can decide that if she can't pitch she won't play, it's all or nothing; she can get into a tailspin because pitching was the most important thing in the world and her life is now a total mess; or she can blame her fate on a particular child or small group for rejecting her.

Or, she can recognize that this thinking isn't helping her, take a pause, breathe, and consider her options. She could consider a pathway toward becoming the pitcher, such as playing a different position, earning the team's trust, and trying out for the position later in the season—or maybe being the substitute pitcher or even pitching occasionally. The latter moves are displays of an efficacious approach to problem-solving. The former choices constitute examples of what we call faulty cognition: demanding, dualizing, drasticating, and demonizing. These are the four sides of D-Mental Block.

Guilt, Grief 'n Grievance Psychology: D-Mental Block

If you tell yourself that "I'm a loser and no one really likes me," then it is likely that you will proceed as if you don't have what it takes. While it's true that "thinking makes it so," there is no implicit guarantee that our thinking will be rational or logical. People frequently engage in faulty cognition

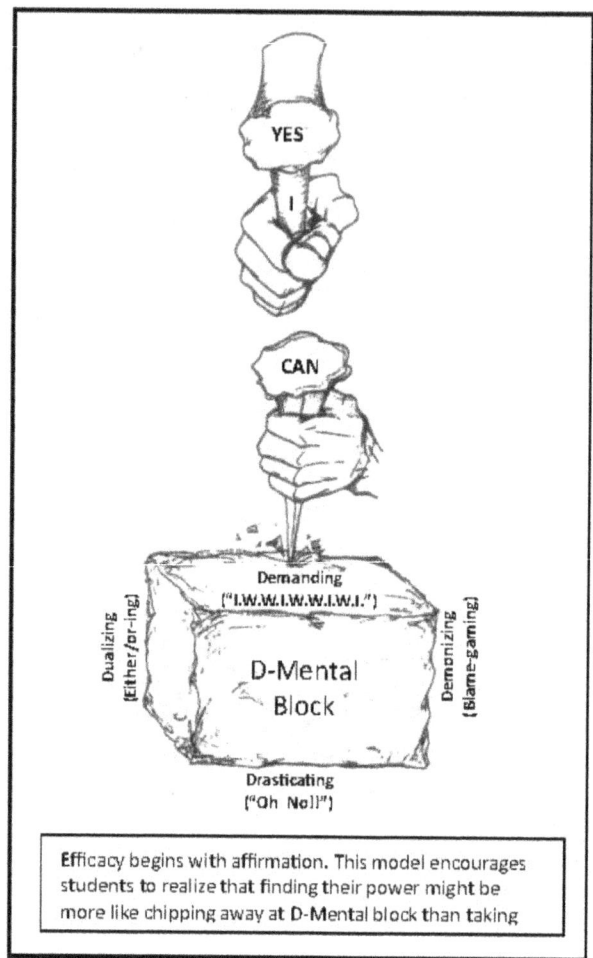

Figure 13.1 D-Mental Block.

(Ellis, 1975); they perseverate, dichotomize, exaggerate, or assign blame. Combined, these four dialectical traps illustrate "D-Mental Block."

D-Tailing D-Mental Block

D-Mental Block is based on a distillation of Albert Ellis's original list of eleven irrational ideas that he believed can corrupt our self-talk. We have further synthesized these items into four major categories or mental cramps. These are essentially internal traps that make up D-Mental Block. While each side of this block appears to operate independently, they are not completely distinct. Additionally, these biases are not always negative. They can be used productively in specific circumstances. Initially with mediation, in a dialectical dialogue, and ultimately as efficacious self-talk, these tendencies can be turned into skills and strategies that help kids to more positively navigate the daily tensions in their lives. In general, they tend to occur in the following order: demanding, dualizing, drasticating, and demonizing.

D-manding

D-mandingness derives from an overarching drive, or biological imperative, to pursue our own survival. At its extreme, an outgrowth of this drive are the self-centered behaviors designed to get our needs met. This is the child who stamps and shouts: "I Want What I Want When I Want . . . IT!" or in shorthand: I.W.W.I.W.W.I.W.I.!

Each of us at our core has an artifact of our primitive, creature-comfort loving, narcissistic, perfectionistic child-self. This persona usually learns to grow up and play nicely in the sandbox of life. However, there are some children in every crowd who will have a greater challenge with achieving an I/we balance. In this child, we see uncompromising, insistent behavior: "It's my way or the highway!"

On the positive side, the passion involved in demandingness can manifest as goal-driven behavior. Imagine a problem-solving group without the high level of energy needed to strive for excellence.

D-ualizing

Dualizing is the tendency to dichotomize or dualize phenomena. It is binary thinking that cuts off exploration and creativity and undermines cooperation by reducing options to either/or.

Our paleo-cortex/amygdala, the seat of our primitive inclinations, is basically a binary processor—crude but effective for supporting survival for early humans in a jungle, yet a disaster in today's more complex and heavily nuanced "world of gray" environment in the Big City. This bi-cameral brain is designed in part to take black-and-white polarized snapshots. However, the perception of objects as dualities creates a dilemma. In an emotionally charged situation, this behavior can escalate and create an uptick in this either/or, night/day thinking. As a result, we are more likely to proceed as if it is either absolutely one thing or the other and we find ourselves facing an artificially forced choice.

However, not all dichotomization is bad. At the appropriate points in a decision-making process, it can actually facilitate results by reducing chaotic thinking and offering clear alternatives.

Drasticating (aka Emotional Dis-regulation, Extremizing, and Dramatizing)

Drasticating is an original Albert Ellis term introduced to describe how we can jump to extreme conclusions, hit the accelerator, and go from zero to sixty in nanoseconds simply because we didn't get what we wanted immediately and chose to believe instead that it is now the end of the world! While some part of this reactivity may be in your neurophysiology, this model stresses how *your* "thinking makes it so!" This means that you have control of the brakes.

That said, projecting the worst-case scenario, without hysteria, can help to make you more strategic in avoiding catastrophic conclusions by creating a firewall to protect against them. Furthermore, calmly envisioning the "worst that could happen" can actually help dial down the potential hysteria.

D-monizing

D-monizing is the tendency to find a scapegoat when things go awry, rather than calmly considering causal factors or even exploring one's own culpability. It is a very natural yet illogical conclusion to the other three sides of D-Mental Block. If you can't get what you want, and you believe it is all doom as a result, and you are now exploding with frustration, the only thing left to do is, of course, deflect and accuse.

D-monizing, in particular, affects efficacy because when this blame gaming occurs, we evade responsibility and pin the tail on some other ass. So, rather than calmly stopping and thinking, "Perhaps, I should reconsider this and try to see where I might've erred?" we find someone or something to blame—even ourselves. Nonetheless, seeking causes outside of our own purview can be a positive strategy. It is a diagnostic approach to effective problem-solving.

Dialogues are a structured learning experience aimed at shifting students' internal dialogue from faulty cognitions to more productive self-talk. In this case, each side of D-Mental Block can sound more like:

Table 13.1 Resolving Dialectical Dilemmas

Instead of:	Ask yourself:
D-manding (I.W.W.I.W.W.I.W.I.)	How can I advocate for my position in a positive way?
D-ualizing (Either/Or-ing)	What might be in the "gray" area that could work?
D-rasticating ("Oh No!!")	What's the worst thing that could happen, really?
D-monizing (Blame-gaming)	What might be my place in causing this, and how might it be fixed?

The Dialectical Dialogue: From Surface Structure to Deep Structure

The Dialectical Dialogue is intended to access emotional modulation and rational thinking; it stimulates self-modifying, self-monitoring, and, ultimately, self-managing. The key point is that children can learn to attend to their self-talk as a signaling system and ask, "What am I saying to myself? Is it healthy or unhealthy?" We advocate for teaching the language and framework of this model to students prior to the need for intervention. When a disturbing event occurs, that is a critical time to surface the resource of efficacy. In this emotionally chaotic space, it is necessary to suspend alarm, pause, breathe, and create a game plan. Given the emotional impact of a stressful event, the search for causes can create distortion, or the application of faulty logic, precisely when it is most important to access our own efficacy and "deal." Building the capacity to do just that is an important outcome of structured engagements, or Dialectical Dialogues. Similar to the exchanges between Socrates and his students, the Dialectical Dialogue surfaces a chain of cause/effect linkages that opens an opportunity to examine our thinking, consider our behavioral choices, and exercise our efficacy. Further, the feedback loop created in this process facilitates access to this key internal resource on future occasions.

The foundation for the Dialectical Dialogue is the Real-Life Survival Game's Fix-It Kit (Jambor, 2000), a needs-driven model designed to give students long-term strategies for success (see Figure 13.2). It is framed around four questions:

- What started it?
- What have you been telling yourself about it?
- How did those thoughts/beliefs make you feel?
- What did you decide to do about it?

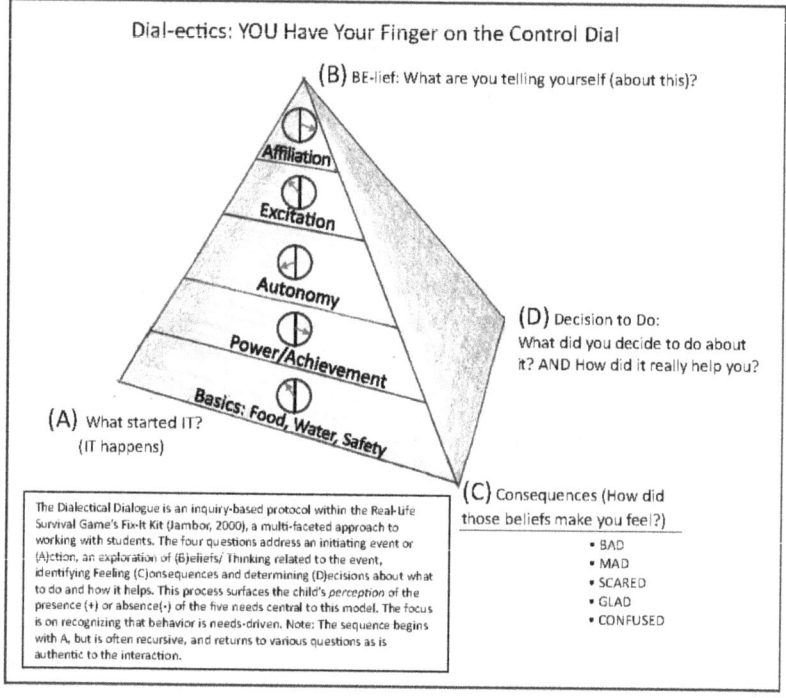

Figure 13.2 Dialectical Dialogue: The Fix-It Kit.

To link past action to future choices, we also add, "How did it really help you?" to the fourth question. This last question is the inquiry that targets efficacy by shining a light on possibilities and positive choices.

A Dialectical Dialogue with DeeDee

DeeDee is referred to the school counselor for being disruptive in class—fidgeting, interrupting, and muttering under her breath trying to agitate her classmates. Her counselor begins the Dialectical Dialogue*, which is familiar to DeeDee from class instruction and previous counseling sessions:

A. **What started it?**
   I joined the softball team and the coach didn't pick me to be the starting pitcher even though I'm the best one for it.
   So to you, the coach blew it and made a bad move.

B. **What were you telling yourself about that?**
It's totally not fair. I'm the best and everybody knows that. She just doesn't like me. She definitely likes Melanie much more.

You think you deserve to be the pitcher. You've got what it takes to bring to the team and the coach just doesn't get it. And, you believe she made her choice not because Melanie plays well, but because she's her favorite. And you really want to be the pitcher.

C. **So, how does that make you feel?**
I'm pissed. And I feel like nobody likes me—the coach or the team. And especially Melanie—because I'm a much better pitcher than her. And everybody really knows that.

So you're feeling like the world isn't fair, it's all the coach's fault and you have no control over the situation.

Yes, and if I can't be the pitcher I'm going to quit the team. That's how I have control.

Okay. Though that is pretty extreme, you love softball. That's all or nothing thinking. So, how about we take a pause, take a breath, and think about this. You're feeling angry because the coach's choices seem unfair, and you want to feel valued and be recognized for your skills. Let's look at the pyramid—you know the buttons "flash" when they need attention. Which of these need buttons are sending out a signal?

Well, I do feel powerless . . .

You know, by quitting you actually lose power, and I'm wondering if your friends button is flashing, too.

Let's think about what you might have control over and consider a plan. What might be some ways you could demonstrate your skills that would feel good to you and provide some steps toward pitching?

DeeDee and her counselor brainstorm some options for her staying on the team, forming stronger relationships with her teammates and perhaps not being the starting pitcher—but pitching from time to time.

(Note: This scenario is an abbreviated example. As in all Cognitive Coaching conversations, the pattern of pause, paraphrase, and probe/inquire would be embedded and applied throughout each phase.)

Toward Self-Directed Learning

Remember, 90% of the game is mental; the other half is physical.
—*Yogi Berra*

Table 13.2 The Dialectical Dialogue

Dialogue Questions	Intention	Process
A. Action: What **started** IT?	To offer the child a safe place to be heard, to share their perspective and to begin processing the event.	Teacher clarifies using paraphrase and inquiry* Listen for and reinforce the message that it is the child's perspective being explored. NOTE: Shaping a child's language helps to shape their feelings and gives them authorship.
B. Belief "What are *telling* yourself (about this)?"	To elicit the child's beliefs about the event and relate them to the purpose/need that is being challenged and to what extent.	Child describes their beliefs about the event—what "needs" button was being pushed? Who, or what, pushed it? NOTE: Pushed buttons trigger vulnerability, so at this stage you are likely to get "push-back."
C. Consequences (resulting feelings) "How did those beliefs make you *feel*? Are you OK or not OK?"	To surface feelings (often primarily negative feelings) to get to the core of the problem—the gist of what is troubling the child. Determining, "are you OK or not OK?" related to which need(s) are being met.	As a result of these interactions, children learn to see their internal dialogue as a signaling system. Their self-talk spiral can reinforce efficacy and create a healthy narrative OR self-defeatism creating an unhealthy narrative. NOTE: This question links to the previous description of beliefs and while it begins as binary (OK or not OK), it launches a fuller array of exploration.
D. Decision "What did you *decide* to do about it? and how did it really help you?"	To explore the action the child took in response to the initial event, and to begin evaluating their choice.	Continue with the process, with the additional question(s): What are you doing now and how is it *really** helping you? *"really" is defined as "How did it help you get your need(s) met?" NOTE: It is important to emphasize here that it was, in fact, the child's choice.

*These skills are applied throughout the process

This chapter offers a method for structuring growth-oriented conversations that promote a higher degree of consciousness, flexibility, and interdependence—requirements for efficacy. To this end, an effective Dialectical Dialogue:

- creates a safe space where students' feelings are validated
- restores a child's control of the narrative
- identifies and debunks faulty cognitions and leads to the construction of reasonable alternatives
- increases awareness of efficacy-building opportunities
- supports recognition and integration of these capabilities for future use

Efficacious individuals of all ages view problems as opportunities, and both failure and success as potential for growth. If we consider these attributes as a focus for education, we can create self-monitoring, self-modifying, self-managing students, who reflect on their behaviors, are attentive to their inner voices, and adjust accordingly toward increasingly positive, productive choices. Students who know they are the authors of their own future.

References

Bandura, A. (1977). Self-efficacy: Toward a unifying theory of behavioral change. *Psychological Review, 84*(2), 191–215.

Bandura, A. (1997). Self-efficacy: *The exercise of control.* W.H. Freeman and Company.

Costa, A., & Garmston, R. (2015). *Cognitive Coaching: Developing self-directed leaders and learners.* Rowan & Littlefield.

Ellis, A., & Harper, R. (1975). *A guide to rational living.* Wilshire Book Company.

Jambor, S. (2000). *The Real-life survival game.* Psi-Illustrated.

Richard, E. M., Diefendorff, J. M., & Martin, J. H. (2006). Revisiting the within-person self-efficacy and performance relation. *Human Performance, 19*(1), 67–87.

Humility and Humanity

14

Humility (p. 142)

Humanity (p. 145)

In Conclusion (p. 147)

Why this chapter?
Often unstated, but always present in constructive interactions are humanity and humility. In this chapter, we elaborate the definitions and specify uses during coaching. These two distinct words, both of Latin origin, share a common theme: they express positive attributes of human behaviors, thoughts, and emotions.

"Humility," derived from the word "humbleness," is deferential, respectful, submissive, self-effacing, unassertive, unpresuming; modest, unassuming, self-deprecating, free from vanity, obsequious, sycophantic, servile; and an absence of arrogance or superiority. It acknowledges one's own limitations, recognizes the worth and perspectives of others, and remains open to continuous learning and growth. Humility promotes empathy and fosters respect for the environment and for the lives, rights, and values of other human beings.

Stemming from the Latin word *humanitas*, "humanity" conveys notions of what it means to be human: culture, kindness, and compassion. It expresses the broader concept of being human and encompasses the virtues and characteristics commonly associated with civil human behavior. It conveys an understanding and concern for the well-being of other individuals and groups. It encourages acts of kindness, generosity, and compassion toward fellow human beings. It emphasizes one's culturally shared experiences, interconnectedness, and peaceful interdependence.

Humility

The only true wisdom is in knowing you know nothing.

—Socrates

In today's world of entertainment, advertising, business, politics, sports, and social media, we live in an era of self-aggrandizement. Fame, riches, vanity, and audacity are often equated with success and power, sometimes claimed by disparaging others in the process. We are encouraged to tout our bravado, our achievements, or our superiority. Hubris, however, should not be confused with efficacious leadership.

Crespo (2023) has identified twenty-one attributes of humility. Nobria (2016) described three types, which we explore here: *moral, intellectual, and personal*.

Moral humility means that we have and live integrity. It is the awareness that no matter how self-assured we are about honoring our morality, ethical values, and principles, we guard being distracted from them when we are in danger, under stress, or at risk (Milgram, 1963). We may lose touch with those values and revert to more punitive behaviors, words, and actions. Although we would like to believe that we would be able to resist the demands of an authority figure, a political leader, or an agency to do harm to others, we may remain vulnerable to succumbing to the situation. Living with integrity will often require us to choose the more difficult path in the short term in order to live by our values and achieve our goals in the long term.

Here is a story about moral humility:

Jeremiah and his three brothers were rescued by an international peacekeeping organization and brought to the United States from Sudan. Jeremiah and his three brothers were placed in foster homes in very different and cold environments. In Sudan, resources were very scarce, and food and water had to be shared in order to survive. Jeremiah's job in a supermarket was to take out the trash, keep the floors clean and remove the old, outdated meats and scarred produce, and place them in the trash bin in the back of the store.

One evening, as the store was closing, a dirty-faced, disheveled, and obviously homeless girl was walking by the trash barrels when Jeremiah was emptying the trash. She reached in and took out a scarred apple and started to eat it. Jeremiah called her and said, "Here is some meat and vegetables that you can have."

Just then the store manager came out and said, "What are you doing? Don't you know we could lose our license for doing that? Who said you could give that food away?"

"Jeremiah said it!" replied the boy.

Personal humility is knowing that it is so much better to let others describe your accomplishments than to parade them yourself. Efficacious leaders of teams and organizations always remember that they are being watched closely for signs of hubris (from the Greek meaning extreme pride and arrogance) and self-importance, which is never an attractive quality.

Our esteemed colleague Jim Knight (2023), surveyed others to find their definitions. Humility involves:

- putting others ahead of ourselves
- listening before talking
- caring, and recognizing how small we are within the awesome grandeur of the cosmos
- being a partner, not a controller (resisting the "don't you know who I am?" syndrome)
- having the courage to change our views based on what we learn from others
- putting aside pride, position, and ego to connect with others and assist them in reaching their desired goals
- praising others' accomplishments and successes

Intellectual humility is the virtue of knowing that no matter how intelligent you think you are, no matter what level of education you have achieved, or how many books you have read, you can always continue to learn from others, from your experiences, and from your mistakes. Inquiring, remaining curious, posing problems, and responding with wonderment and awe to the beauties and mysteries of life and the universe are habits displayed and practiced by humble people throughout their lifetime. True wisdom comes from understanding our own limits—recognizing what we don't know—so we can continue learning. By being open-minded about our intellectual shortcomings, we increase our chances of growing intellectually.

Personal assessment: the degree to which I plan to become even more mindful of this quality in myself.

Can we learn to become more humble?

We believe that efficacious learners are on a continuous journey of self-improvement. They:

- embrace a growth mindset and recognize, that they have room for growth and that there is always something new to learn,
- remain open to feedback and constructive criticism,
- cultivate gratitude by regularly acknowledging and appreciating the contributions of other individuals and groups, remembering that they are part of a larger community and that their accomplishments are a result of collective efforts,
- practice active listening: truly listen to others without value judgments or interruptions,
- Seek to understand and honor their biases, perspectives, opinions, and experiences (Knight 2023),
- acknowledge and learn from their own mistakes and limitations,

seek feedback, learn from others, and take responsibility for their actions. *Think lightly of yourself and deeply of the world. (Miyamoto Musashi)*

You may know you're getting better at being humble if you:

- find yourself less defensive in the face of criticism
- are less likely to put others down to elevate yourself
- become more open-minded and willing to consider different perspectives and ideas
- receive feedback from those around you that you are demonstrating more humility
- accept your limitations and make an effort to make the world a better place without wanting to take all the credit.

Personal assessment: the degree to which I plan to become even more mindful of this quality in myself.

CAUTION: Humility has nothing to do with being meek, weak, indecisive, or spineless. Being humble does not mean that you don't have ideas of your

Table 14.1 Rate your humility quotient

1	2	3	4	5
A bit				A lot

own, that you are a follower rather than a leader, or that you will succumb to other people's ideas and desires. It *does* mean that you honor others' values, thoughts, and feelings.

A quote from Simon Sinek:

> The true price of leadership is the willingness to place the needs of others above your own. Great leaders truly care about those they are privileged to lead and understand that the true cost of leadership privilege comes at the expense of self-interest.

So, no matter how efficacious you become (and the intent of this book is to help you become even more so), always remain humble.

Humanity

In today's interconnected and globalized world, it is now commonplace for people of dissimilar worldviews, faiths, and races to live side by side. It is a matter of great urgency, therefore, that we find ways to cooperate with one another in a spirit of mutual acceptance and respect.

We often hear that whenever a culture has an abundance of anything, there are usually many names for it. For example, Inuit people have many words for snow, Italians have many words for pasta, and Hawaiians have many words for wind. The ancient Greeks had seven different words for love, and each held different meanings (Wikipedia). Following this, we explore four of the main Greek words for love: *Philia*, *Eros*, *Storge*, and *Agape*.

- *Philia* refers to the love between close friends or brothers—brotherly love.
- *Eros* refers to the love found in romantic relationships—passion, romance, and intimacy.
- *Storge* is the love between family members—a strong bond shared between parents and their children.
- *Agape* is unconditional, empathetic, universal love toward humanity itself. It involves caring for, serving, and loving others without expecting anything in return—helping others selflessly—with

Table 14.2 Rate your humanity quotient

1	2	3	4	5
A bit				A lot

humility. In its highest form, it is the foundation of productive teams, great nations, diverse societies, close families, and, of course, efficacious schools.

NOTE: In this section on humanity, we will mention love often. The reader must remember that it is the Agape form of love on which we are focusing.

How we learn to become more humane:

- Seek to understand and empathize with the emotions and experiences of others. Show compassion, kindness, support, and love.
- Volunteer and engage in acts of service to your community—by helping those in need, you will develop a profound sense of your part in humanity.
- Surround yourself with others who are from diverse backgrounds, cultures, ethnicities, and beliefs. Seek to befriend and understand them.
- Deliberately engage in conversations that challenge your assumptions and stretch your perspectives on the world's problems and issues. "Help me understand how you've come to that conclusion."
- Employ the language of love (agape) in your interactions, your correspondence, and your own inner language.
- Employ touch like high-fives, handshakes, and fist bumps (when consensual and culturally appropriate)!

Developing these traits is an ongoing, lifelong process of learning that requires consistent effort. Be patient and embrace mistakes as opportunities to learn and strive for continuous growth (Frost, 2024).

How might we know if we're getting more humane?

1. decreasing fighting and increasing dialogue as a way of solving problems
2. decline in violent crime, reduction of wars, and international conflicts
3. increased empathy with more people able to understand and appreciate the emotions and conditions of others
4. greater awareness and interest in the protection and preservation of our delicate environment
5. increased advocacy for equal rights and justice for the impoverished and marginalized groups
6. increased philanthropic efforts and donations to help those who are needy and less fortunate
7. increased funding and interest in accessing education for all
8. support for advancing the sciences that lead to improving the quality of life

9. stronger feelings of safety and protection
10. language we hear within ourselves, from our leaders as well as parents, teachers, and students demonstrates more love, kindness, and compassion

Listening with understanding and empathy creates agape. Here are some quotations:

> For one human being to love another: that is perhaps the most difficult of all of our tasks (Abrams et al., 2016).
>
> The world for which we all work is but preparation (Rainer Maria Rilke).
>
> Understanding and loving are inseparable (Erich Fromm).

There is but one preparation for the task of loving: deep listening—the best tool we have for coaching each other in the agility and endurance necessary for sustaining a true and lasting love, the work of both passionate interest in the inner world of the other and profound knowledge. True curiosity is a form of love because, as the great Zen teacher Thich Nhat Hanh (2006) so plainly and poignantly put it, "understanding is love's other name."

Personal assessment: the degree to which I plan to become even more mindful of this quality in myself.

In conclusion

Though distinct in their meanings, humility and humanity both reflect aspects of positive human qualities. *Humility* builds empathy, selflessness, and continuous learning, and *humanity* builds love and peace. These values allow us to accept life as it sometimes is—broken and imperfect, even as we aspire for a better life. They highlight our unique abilities to find joy, embrace modesty, and show kindness and compassion to others, ultimately contributing to a more harmonious, thoughtful, and loving world. They imply that we humans can become even more so.

> My humanity is bound up in yours, so we can only be human together (Desmond Tutu) (Abrams et al., 2016).

And really, that is the deepest and most meaningful reason Cognitive Coaching is practiced and why it persists.

References

Abrams, D., Dalai Lama, & Tutu, D. (2016) *The book of joy: Lasting happiness in a changing world.* Random House.

Crespo, R. (2023, October). The top 21 attributes of a humble person. *Minimalism made simple.*

Frost, A. (2024, February 12). The love languages at work: The 5 languages of appreciation. *Success Magazine.*

Garmston, R. J., & Wellman, B. M. (2012) *The adaptive school: A sourcebook for developing collaborative groups* (2nd ed.). Rowman & Littlefield Publishers.

Hanh, T. H. (2006). *True love: A practice for awakening the heart.* Shambhala Publications, Inc. Boulder, CO. SBN: 1590301889.

Knight, J. (2023, November 1). Five habits of humility. *Educational Leadership, 81*(3), 78–79.

Milgram, S. (1963). Behavioral study of obedience. *Journal of Abnormal and Social Psychology, 67*(4), 371–378.

Nohria, N. (2016). The three types of humility that impact your leadership. *Leading blog* April 14, 2020. Graduation address.

Glossary

Agency: In psychology, agency is associated with a person's ability to influence their own life circumstances and outcomes. In broader discussions, agency can also relate to empowerment, autonomy, and the ability to exercise one's rights and responsibilities.

Autonomy: A state of being self-governing, self-directing, feelings of freedom, and moral independence.

Cognitive Coaching: A professional development process aimed at enhancing the cognitive skills of educators, helping them reflect on their practices, locating and accessing applicable internal resources, and improving their teaching methodologies. It promotes self-directed learning through structured conversations between a coach and an educator, focusing on facilitating higher-order thinking, problem-solving, and effective decision-making.

The process usually involves three main phases:

1. Planning: The coach and the educator collaboratively set goals and plan lessons or instructional strategies.
2. Observation: The coach observes the educator in action, which provides insights into teaching practices.
3. Reflecting: After the observation, there is a debriefing session where they discuss what happened, analyze outcomes, and identify areas for improvement.

Collective efficacy: A group's shared belief in its collective capabilities to organize and execute courses of action required to produce given levels of attainment (Bandura, 1997, p. 477). John Hattie emphasized that for teacher collective efficacy to be effective, individuals must share a firm conviction that the ideas generated as a collaborative effort are perhaps greater than those generated by an individual. Collective efficacy is strengthened when increases in student achievement are realized based on the sustained efforts of high-powered teams within schools.

Efficacy: Formerly, we considered efficacy to be on a par with the four States of Mind. Currently, we are considering that when one is behaving efficaciously, these states of mind—craftsmanship, interdependence, flexibility, and consciousness—are activated as resources. Engaging in cause-and-effect thinking, spending energy on tasks, setting challenging goals, persevering in the face of barriers and occasional failure, and forecasting future performances accurately. Efficacy is the belief that one's efforts regarding the achievement of a specific goal will result in satisfactory completion.

The pursuit of efficacy activates the States of Mind listed here:

- **Consciousness:** The human capacity to represent information about what is happening outside and inside the body in such a way that it can be evaluated and acted upon by the body. To be conscious is to be aware of one's thoughts, feelings, points of view, and behaviors and the effect they have on the self and others.
- **Craftsmanship:** The drive to hone, refine, and constantly work for improvement. Includes striving for precision, elegance, refinement, and fidelity.
- **Flexibility:** The capacity to simultaneously perceive from multiple perspectives and to endeavor to change, adapt, and expand the repertoire of response patterns. Involves humor, creativity, risk-taking, and adaptability.
- **Interdependence:** The need for reciprocity, belonging, and connectedness. The inclination to become one with the larger system and community. The group contributes learning to the individual and the individual contributors learning to the group.

(Note: At the time of this writing, we are considering that efficacy encompasses the engagement of all five States of Mind especially in volatile, uncertain, complex, and ambiguous situations.)

Holonomy: A person's cognitive capacity to accept the concept that he or she is whole in terms of self and yet subordinate to a higher system. The condition of being an *independent* individual and an *interdependent* member of a group simultaneously. Humans have an internal drive for self-assertiveness which may conflict with a yearning to be in harmony with others and the surrounding environment. A holonomic person, therefore, is one who possesses the capabilities to transcend this dichotomous relationship, maintaining self-directedness while acting both independently and interdependently. Holonomic people recognize their capacities to self-regulate and to be informed by the norms, values, and concerns of a larger system. Of equal importance, they recognize their capacity to influence the values, norms, and practices of the entire system. The ability to function as a member of the whole while still maintaining separateness.

Identity: A mental model we construct of ourselves as unique individuals, constructed from the meanings we make of our interactions with others and how we perceive that others see us.

Interdependence: The human need for reciprocity, belonging, and connectedness. The inclination to become one with the larger system and community. (See also: States of Mind.)

Leadership: Not a role, but as a complex set of skills, values, and principles dedicated to advancing self-directed learning, autonomy, holonomy, individual and collective professional growth, and student development.

Principles: A fundamental truth or proposition that serves as the foundation for a system of belief or behavior or for a chain of reasoning. Cognitive Coaching could be said to include the principles of self-directed learning, all communication has meaning, the unconscious is always listening, and humans yearn for completeness. Cognitive Coaching emphasizes the role of metacognition, encouraging teachers to think about their thinking and understand their decision-making processes. It ultimately aims to create a culture of continuous improvement and professional growth in educational settings. For example, a person acquiring the mindset of presuming positive intention can, by reminding oneself of this perception when engaging with others, make this mindset permanent.

Self-efficacy: An individual's belief in their capacity to act in the ways necessary to reach specific goals. The concept was originally proposed by the psychologist Albert Bandura in 1977. Self-efficacy affects every area of human endeavor. By determining the beliefs a person holds regarding their power to affect situations, self-efficacy strongly influences both the power a person actually has to face challenges competently and the choices a person is most likely to make. A strong sense of self-efficacy promotes human accomplishment and personal well-being. A person with high self-efficacy views challenges as things that are supposed to be mastered rather than threats to avoid. These individuals are able to recover from failure faster and are more likely to attribute failure to a lack of effort. They approach threatening situations with the belief that they can control them.

Skills: The practice of Cognitive Coaching includes these skills: non directive communication, trust, rapport, reflective listening, mediative questioning, presuming positive intention, and metacognition. (Awareness or analysis of one's own learning or thinking processes.)

Values: Individual beliefs that motivate people to act one way or another. They serve as a guide for human behavior. Generally, people are predisposed to adopt the values that they are raised with. People also tend to believe that those values are "right" because they are the values of their individual culture. New values can be acquired through repetitive experience and reflection. Values of Cognitive Coaching include self-directedness, continuous learning, developing personal resources, and assuming positive intentions.

Self-directedness: The ability of an individual to manage their own learning, behaviors, and actions without needing extensive guidance or direction from others. It encompasses skills such as goal-setting, motivation, self-monitoring, and the ability to make decisions independently. A self-directed person is efficacious, typically takes initiative, is proactive about seeking out information or resources, and assumes responsibility for their own progress and outcomes.

States of Mind: Previously we introduced and described five States of Mind: *efficacy, flexibility, consciousness, craftsmanship,* and *interdependence.* (See the entry for "**Efficacy**" above.)

Philogelos: The Greek word for people who love laughter and humor.

Further Reading

We are extremely grateful to the authors who contributed to this book, but we wanted to give special thanks to Dr. Jenny Edwards who has maintained a clearinghouse for studies about Cognitive Coaching and has consistently been an important contributor to our learning. For a full report of her research, refer to chapter 13 in *Cognitive Coaching: A Foundation for Renaissance Schools*. Dr. Edwards can be reached at **jedwards@fielding.edu** or **jedwards23@yahoo.com**.

We are also indebted to our colleagues Laura Lipton and Bruce Wellman for increasing our understanding of paraphrasing. To deepen your understanding of their work and order their books, visit www.Mivavia.com.

For a more complete view of **adaptive change**, please see *Complexity Leadership Theory: An Interactive Perspective on Leading in Complex Adaptive Systems*. http://digitalcommens.unl.edu/managementfacpub.

For information concerning Cognitive Coaching seminars, leadership training, products, and other services, contact the Thinking Collaborative:

Mail: PO Box 630860 Highlands Ranch, CO 80163
E-mail: CCClj@Aol.com
Phone: (303) 683-6146
Online: www.cognitivecoaching.com

Index

The 5th Discipline (Senge) 108

Aaker, Jennifer 31
adaptive change xiii–xiv
   complexity leadership orientation xii
   complex nonlinear system xii
   dynamic systems xiv–xv
   technical changes xiv
adaptive leadership xi; *see also* adaptive change
   avoid adaptive work xvi–xvii
   holding environment xvi
   technical *vs.* adaptive change xvi
   tension xv
The Adaptive School (Garmston and Wellman) viii, xiv
Adaptive School (Garmston and Wellman) xiv
adaptivity 123–4
Adler, Alfred 130
Adult learning theory 94
adverse childhood experiences (ACEs) 61
Agape 145–6
Amerson, Theresa 92, 93
Anderson, Robert 116
The Answer to How Is Yes (Block) 104
The Anxious Micromanager xviii
Ardern, Jacinda 62
Ariav, T. 11
attention deficit hyperactivity disorder (ADHD) 37
authentic paraphrase 120, 121
autism 37
autobiographical listening 119
Awakuni, G. H. 12

Bagdonas, Naomi 31
Batt, E. G. 7
Beeson, R. 11
Bell, J. 6
Benioff, Marc 63
Bjerken, K. S. 11
Block, Peter 104, 105
Botzer, I. 11
Bridges, Ruby 53
Brosnan, P. 10

Career Advancement and Development of Recruits and Experienced (CADRE) 6
Carter, Jimmy 66
Catmull, Ed 107
The Centro Internacional Teresiano-Sanjuanista (CITeS) 82
Checa, Rafael 82
Christian Spiritual Accompaniment 79–80
   Cognitive Coaching 80–1
   formators 84–5
   in Mexico 81–2
   Pontifical Faculty of Teresianum in Rome 82
   University of Mysticism in Avila 82–4
Clarke, John 35
Clinard, L. M. 11
clinical supervision model 116, 117
Cogan, Morris 116, 117
Cognitive Coaching vii, viii, 2
   context 122–3
   efficacy 105–6
   eleven outcomes of implementing 4–5

abilities to reflect and
    think 9–11
benefits for administrators 14–15
benefits for professionals 15
choice of profession 11–12
collaboration 13
higher levels of implementation
    of innovations 6–8
personal growth 14
position satisfaction 11–12
professional cultures 12–13
professional growth 13–14
professionals efficacy
    development 8–9
successful induction 5–6
formal dyadic interactive
    strategy 122
metacognitive skills 118–20
mission 118
neuro-biochemical effects 120–1
nineteen recommendations for
    implementing 16–17
    assign cognitive coaches 22
    CBAM tools 18
    coaching skills uses 20
    coach *vs.* evaluate
        employees 21
    develop Five States of
        Mind 21–2
    develop self-directedness 19
    employees benefit 18
    establish long-term system-wide
        support 17
    establish trusting
        relationships 19
    identity of a mediator of
        thinking 20
    importance of reflection 19
    informal basis 20–1
    managers support 17
    norms of collaboration 18
    organizational learning 20
    policies in larger
        environment 21
    structure time 20
    variety of contexts 21
    voluntary participation 19

persists 123–6
research-based strategy 117–18
roots of 116–17
vision 118
We Can't Always Coach 121
work 122–3
Cognitive Coaching (Art and
    Bob) vii
*Cognitive Coaching: Greater Rational,
    Emotional and Spiritual
    Intelligence* 82
Collaborative for Academic, Social
    and Emotional Learning
    (CASEL) 62
competence 45–49, 66, 72, 125
complex adaptive system
    (CAS) xiii
complexity leadership theory xi,
    xii
Concerns-Based Adoption Model
    (CBAM) 16, 18
Conroy, J. 11
Costa, Arthur vii, 106
Cox, J. H. 9, 10
Creating Talent Density 107
Creativity (Catmull) 107
Crespo, R. 142

Dalio, Ray 64
de Cetina, Diego 83, 85
Dewey, John 73
Diaz, K. A. 6, 7
DiGangi, Julia xviii
disequilibrium 120
diversity 53–4
    create sense of inclusion and
        belonging 54
    five Tibetan stages to solve
        complex problems 58–9
    organizational culture 55–6
    stronger work groups 54–5
    working together in diverse
        workplace 56–8
Dougherty, P. A. 13
Dwyer, M. 11
Dyer, John 30, 35, 88, 89
dyslexia 37

Edmondson, Amy   107
Educational Leadership (Costa and Garmston)   2, 115
Edwards, Jenny   2, 80, 82, 83, 117
efficacious leadership   xvii, 45–6
　DeeDee   136–7
　Dialectical Dialogue   135–6
　D-Mental Block   131–2
　　demanding   133
　　demonizing   134–5
　　drasticating   134
　　dualizing   133–4
　D-Tailing D-Mental Block   132–3
　engagement   48–9
　growing collective efficacy in teams   xix, xxi–xxii
　journey   xxiii
　kickoff   46
　promoting self-efficacy in others   xix, xxi
　relationships   50–1
　　two final thoughts on   51–2
　scaffolding positive self-talk   129–31
　second facilitator   49–50
　self-directed learning   137–9
　self-managing   xviii–xix
　self-modifying   xix, xx–xxi
　self-monitoring   xviii, xix–xx
　vulnerability   47–8
efficacy   129–30
Eichholz, K. F.   xiii, xvi
Ellis, Albert   132, 134
Emerson, Ralph Waldo   126
emotional intelligence (EI)   41, 61–4, 66
Eros   145

fascia   73
FeedForward   105
Fix-It Kit   135, 136
Four Pivots (Ginwright)   56

Garmston, Bob   viii, xii, 42, 85
Garmston, Robert   vii, 95
Gell-Mann, Murray   viii, xiii
Ginwright, Shawn   56

Göker, M. U.   8
Göker, S. D.   5, 8, 13, 14
Goldhammer, Robert   116
Goldman Sachs   64
Goldsmith, Marshall   105–107, 110
González Del Castillo, A.   5, 10
grief   xvii
Grinder, Michael   121
Grochocki, J.   13

Hall, Doug   30
Hanh, Thich Nhat   147
Harts, Minda   57
Hattie, John   xxii
Hauserman, C. P.   6, 9
Hayes, Carolee   35
health care   87–8
　history   88–93
　recommendations   93–5
Heifetz, Ronald   xi, xv, xvi, xvii
Helgesen, Sally   110
Helping (Schein)   106
Henry, Barbara   53
High Expectations Teaching (Saphier)   106
holonomy   116
Hsieh, Tony   66
humanity   116, 145–6
　agape   147
　being humane   146–7
　positive human qualities   147
Humble Inquiry (Schein)   105
humility   116, 141
　being humble   144–5
　intellectual   143–4
　moral   142–3
　personal   143
　positive human qualities   147
Hunter, C.   10
Hunter, Madeline   117
Hyerle, D.   4

IDEO   65
Inclusify (Johnson)   110
inquisitive listening   119
International Congress of Spiritual Theology   82

International Trade Association (ITA)   35
Interpersonal Confirmation Theory   89, 90
Irons, N. A.   7

Jaberzadeh, Richard   39
Jaede, M.   10
Johnson, J. B.   9, 17, 18
Johnson, Stephanie   110

Kallick, Bena   72
Kibben, Katrina   57
Knight, Jim   143
Kornfield, Jack   54
Krancher, Glenn   40

Lane, Deb   41
Laycock, K.   11
Leader2Leader (L2) Leadership Pilot Program   6
leadership theory   xi, xii
Leigh, K.   10
Liebmann, R.   15
Linsky, Marty   xi
Lipton, Laura   121
The Little Engine That Could (Piper)   xx

Maccise, Camillo   80
Maslach Burnout Inventory   91
McNamer, Bridget   40
Menlo Innovations   108
Metacognitive Awareness Inventory (MAI)   9
Miller, George   108
mind-body awareness   71–2, 75
  culture of connection   78
  Habits of Mind   73–4
    client's perspective   75
    institute of   77
  Habits of Movement   73–4
    eight habits of   76
    trainer's perspective   74
  real strength   76
  tuning up sensors   72–3
Minor, L.   11
Mirón, L.   11

music education   97
  influences focus and mood   100–1
  prepare students for performance   97–9

Nadella, Satya   62
National Board Certification   7, 10
neurodivergent   37–8
  adaptation   38–9
  Cognitive Coaching alignment   39–40
  conscious application of introspection   41–2
  distributed   40–1
  definitions   38
  natural cognitive awareness   38–9
  neurodiverse leaders   43
  transformative potential   43–4
neurosignature   38
neurotypical   38
Nooyi, Indra   65

paleo-cortex/amygdala   133
Pastoral Care of Spirituality   82
Pavlock, K. C.   14
Person-Centered Approach   85
Philia   145
Philogelos   29–32
pinch of reality   xvii
Pixar   107
Polman, Paul   65
prosocial learning   62
  educator efficacy   66
  emotional intelligence   62–3
  leadership team   65
  New Normal   62
  prosocial leadership   66
  social and emotional learning   62–3
  thrive learning   63–5
    envision   66–7
  work environments   63–5
    envision   66–7

Reed, L. A.   12, 14, 17, 18
Reflection-FOR-Action   104
Reflection-IN-Action   104
Reflection-ON-Action   104

Reflective Pedagogical Thinking
  Instrument (RPT)   9
Rennick, L. W.   8
Reverse Las Vegas Effect   108
Rogers, Carl   79, 85
Rogers, W. T.   6, 9, 14, 15
Rosberg, Bengt   41
Rosberg, Diana   42
Royal College of Physicians and
  Surgeons   91

Salcedo, Don Francisco de   83
Sándigo, A. M.   8
Santa Cruz elementary school   65
Saphier, Jon   106
Schein, Edgar   105, 106
Schon, Donald   104
self-managing   118
self-modifying   118
self-monitoring   118
Senge, Peter   108
Sheltered Instruction Observation
  Protocol (SIOP)   6–7
Sheridan, Richard   108
Sherman, Eryn   38
Sills-Maerov, Margie   35, 88, 89
Simoneau, Carol   35
Sinek, Simon   145
Skytt, J.   6
Skytt, J. K.   9
social and emotional competence
  (SEC)   66
social and emotional learning
  (SEL)   61, 64

solution listening   119
Stanley, Stacie   56
states of mind   viii, 106
  consciousness   107–8
  craftsmanship   108–9
  flexibility   106–7
  interdependence   109–10
Steiner, A.   6
Storge   145
strategic questioning   104
Stroot, S.   10
Suroweicki, James   109

Tennison, R.   17
This Is Water (Wallace)   55
total quality management (TQM)   109
Train Awareness Performance
  (TAP)   71, 73

WakeMed Hospitals   92
Walczak, B.   10
Wallace, David Foster   55
Walsh, James J.   31
Weatherford, D.   21
Weatherford, N.   21
Wellman, Bruce   viii, xii, 121
Wheatley, Margaret   57, 58
Wilcoxen, C.   6
Wisdom of Crowds (Suroweicki)   109
Wooten Burnett, S. W.   8

Yule, K.   11

Zebro, E. J.   72, 75, 76

About the Contributors

Wendy Baron is a teacher, author, coach, and leader in education. Wendy cofounded Santa Cruz/Silicon Valley New Teacher Project, a COE mentoring program for beginning teachers, and New Teacher Center, a nonprofit dedicated to improving student learning. Wendy served on the CA Department of Education's Task Force, developing resources for the Greater Good Science Center, and currently works with school leaders, teachers, counselors, and mental health clinicians supporting a systems approach to social-emotional-academic development and schools as centers of wellbeing.

John Clarke is a training associate with Thinking Collaborative, providing Cognitive Coaching and Adaptive Schools/Organizations seminars in Canada, the United States, Australia, and South Korea. He is also the director for Coaching and Design with Thought Architects. John provides multifaceted consulting and coaching resources to educational, corporate, and health care clients to develop adaptive, resilient, and impactful professional organizations. As a former school principal and a communications consultant, John's primary focus has always been on creating and sustaining safe, positive, and productive work cultures.

Phil Echols, PhD, serves as an organizational development and diversity specialist for one of North Carolina's large healthcare providers and is a global consultant for educational and healthcare institutions. Dr. Echols holds a Doctorate in Education from Northeastern University in Organizational Leadership. He has presented sessions for ASCD, Learning Forward, and the Near East South Asia Council of Overseas Schools. His work is anchored in his mission to inspire and support individuals and groups in doing and being their best.

Jenny Edwards, PhD, teaches in the Leadership for Change doctoral program at Fielding Graduate University. She wrote *Cognitive Coaching SM: A Synthesis of the Research* (Thinking Collaborative, 2025), which is in its 19th edition, and *Inviting Students to Learn: 100 Tips for Talking Effectively with Your Students* (ASCD, 2010). She is a training associate for

Cognitive Coaching and Adaptive Schools and has presented them in Italian, Spanish, and English. She lives in Evergreen, Colorado. She can be reached at jedwards@fielding.edu.

Luis J. Gonzalez, a Carmelite priest, was born in Guadalajara, Mexico. He has a PhD in spiritual theology, a PhD in psychology, and a PhD in Rogerian counseling. Since 2000, he has conducted trainings in Cognitive Coaching and Adaptive Schools around the world for priests, nuns, and laypeople. He has written eighty-six books. He leads a program called "Formators for the Mystical Experience" at the University of the Mystics in Ávila, Spain, that is based on Cognitive Coaching℠ and Theology.

Stephen O. Jambor, PhD, is a child advocate and counseling psychologist with more than thirty-five years of experience working with students with special needs. Dr. Jambor is both a certified school psychologist and school counselor and holds a PhD in educational psychology from Fordham University. Steve has worked with "children of all ages" as well as graduate students at Fordham University. He presently coordinates a Substack, Psi-Illustrated, which focuses on applying psychological theories to current provocative topics.

Bena Kallick, PhD, is an international author, consultant, and cofounder of the Institute for Habits of Mind. She has devoted her career to improving education through self-directed learning, supporting students in developing their own thought processes, and learning to engage critical and creative thinking using Habits of Mind. She is a leader in helping teachers navigate the transition from outdated learning processes to thought-filled opportunities for students to develop agency in the pursuit of global problem-solving.

Delores B. Lindsey, PhD, a former teacher, assistant principal, principal, and county office of education administrator and retired associate professor of education at California State University, San Marcos, California, focuses on developing culturally proficient leaders. She and her husband, Randall, cofounded the Center for Culturally Proficient Educational Practice. Delores has published numerous Corwin bestsellers, including *Leading While Female (2020)* and *My Leading While Female Journey* (2023) with Dr. Trudy Arriaga and Dr. Stacie Stanley.

Laura E. Lipton, EdD, is an international consultant whose writing, research, keynotes, and seminars focus on effective and innovative instructional practices, as well as building professional and organizational capacities for enhanced learning. Laura is an author and coauthor of numerous publications related to organizational and professional development. During her career, Laura has engaged with school districts, public and independent schools, departments of education, and international agencies, conducting workshops on organizational and group development and growth-oriented supervisory and mentoring practices.

Bridget McNamer is passionate about helping adventurous people enhance their sense of the possible. I have brought this passion to my work with school leaders, social entrepreneurs, philanthropists, corporate executives, and young people. I currently serve as Chief Navigation Officer for Sidecar Counsel, which aims to bring more women into leadership roles in schools, enhance their leadership capacities once there, and cultivate an environment where women in these schools—and thereby all members of the school community—can thrive.

Diana Rosberg is passionate about supporting educators and leaders in realizing their vision and potential. With more than three decades of experience in international education, she works with schools worldwide on leadership development, strategic planning, accreditation, curriculum design, and policy development aligned with a school's vision. She also supports women expats in taking control of their financial lives and building financial freedom through Financing While Female, the coaching service she founded. Diana is proudly autistic.

William Sommers, PhD, is a learner, author, and leadership coach. As the director of Stakeholder Centered Coaching for Educators and cofounder of www.learningomnivores.com, he has authored over fifteen books. A certified coach in SCC, Polarity Management, and Conflict Management, he conducts workshops and writes blogs and book summaries. Dr. Sommers has experience in graduate faculties, served as a program director for an adolescent chemical dependency treatment center, and was involved with the Lian Dante Foundation for Social Justice.

Stacie L. Stanley, EdD, is superintendent of Saint Paul Public Schools and previously served as the superintendent of Edina Public Schools and associate superintendent of Eden Prairie Schools. Her roles included teacher, principal, and director of curriculum. Stacie is an advocate for youth voice and equitable learning. She coauthored *Leading While Female: A Culturally Proficient*

Response for Gender Equity and is a contributing author to *Innovative Voices in Education: Engaging Diverse Communities*. She is committed to ensuring women, especially women of color, are positioned to move into leadership.

Michael Tonkin is CEO of Tonka Learning, framing his role as chief educator, learner, strategist, coach, and ambassador. Over nearly three decades, he has led transformational capability and culture projects in 50+ countries and industries. Formerly CEO of Maura Fay Learning and Head of Global Learning at Cotton On Group, he has also run his own consulting firm. Michael's work has helped organizations boost performance, win global learning awards, and lead corporate academies with budgets exceeding $30 million.

EJ Zebro, CCSP, has over twenty-five years of experience in functional movement. He studied Exercise Science at the University of Delaware while playing D1 soccer. As a certified Chiropractic Sports Physician, he served as a strength and conditioning coach and developed the TAP fascial manipulation methodology. This approach enhances physical performance, reduces injury rates, and speeds recovery. EJ aims to help clients tap into their internal experiences and understand their bodies' movements, supporting their journey to thrive at every life stage.

Diane P. Zimmerman, PhD, has spent her life helping people and organizations learn, grow, and thrive. She served as a teacher, principal, and superintendent, and coauthored numerous journal articles and five books on leadership. Whether in schools or print, Diane's work has focused on building teacher efficacy through knowledge partnerships—collaborations that nurture the deep skills of learning. Her mission has been to create lasting knowledge legacies: communities that preserve wisdom and pass it on to those who follow.

Kendall Zoller, EdD, is an author, educator, researcher, and global consultant specializing in communicative intelligence, leadership, storytelling, and presentation/facilitation skills. He has worked with hundreds of schools and organizations across twenty-five countries and virtually in over eighty. His books include *The Choreography of Presenting* (2024), *HeartSpace* (2021), and *Voices Leading from the Ecotone* (2019). Kendall is president of Sierra Training Associates and a graduate faculty member at CSU Dominguez Hills. Contact him at kvzollerci@gmail.com.